Edexcel GCSE

History B

Schools History Project

Life in Germany c1919–c1945 (Option 2C)

Steve Waugh

Series editor: Angela Leonard

A PEARSON COMPANY

Published by Pearson Education Limited, a company incorporated in England and Wales, having its registered office at Edinburgh Gate, Harlow, Essex, CM20 2JE. Registered company number: 872828

www.heinemann.co.uk

Edexcel is a registered trade mark of Edexcel Limited

Text © Pearson Education Ltd 2009
First published 2009

13 12 11 10
10 9 8 7 6 5 4

British Library Cataloguing in Publication Data
A catalogue record for this book is available from the British Library.

ISBN 978 1 846904 44 8

Produced and edited by Florence Production Ltd, Stoodleigh, Devon
Designed by Pearson Education Ltd
Typeset and illustrated by HL Studios, Long Hanborough, Oxford
Original illustrations © Pearson Education Ltd 2009
Cover design by Pearson Education Ltd
Picture research by Maria Joannou
Cover photo © AKG Images / Collection Archiv f. Kunst & Geschichte
Printed in China (CTPS / 04)

Acknowledgements
The author and publisher would like to thank the following individuals and organisations for permission to reproduce material:

Photographs
Alamy Images / INTERFOTO Pressebildagentur pp. 42, 59; Alamy Images / Mary Evans Picture Library p. 88; Alamy Images / Photos 12 p. 69; Alamy Images / The Print Collector / Art Media p. 17; AKG Images pp. 2, 18, 25, 26, 33, 42, 45, 62, 81, 92; AKG Images / Collection Archiv f.Kunst & Geschichte p 89; AKG Images / Ullstein Bild p. 65; BPK pp. 3, 13, 14, 54, 70, 72; Bridgeman Art Library / Deutsches Historisches Museum, Berlin, Germany / DHM Arne Psille p. 71; Bridgeman Art Library / Kunstgewerbe Museum, Zurich, Switzerland / Archives Charmet p. 11; Bridgeman Art Library / Laket Museum, Essen, Germany / Archives Charmet p. 49; Bridgeman Art Library / Private Collection / Archives Charmet pp. 68, 84; Bridgeman Art Library / Private Collection / Peter Newark Military Pictures pp. 23, 53, 77; Bundesarchiv p. 58; Corbis / Austrian Archives p. 51; Corbis / Bettmann p. 37; Corbis / Hulton-Deutsch Collection p. 24; Corbis / Stapleton Collection p. 102; David King p. 55; Fotolibra pp. 2, 8, 20, 68, 82, 96; Getty Images / Dmitri Kessel / Time Life Pictures p. 62; Getty Images / Hulton Archive p. 12; Getty Images / Popperfoto p. 59; Mary Evans Picture Library pp. 5, 72; Photoshot pp. 42, 62, 63, 57; Photoshot / UPPA pp. 16, 48–49; Professor Bytwerk pp. 68, 75; Rex Features p. 21; Rex Features / Roger-Viollet p. 91; Topfoto p. 43; Topfoto / Roger-Viollet p. 31; Topfoto / Ullstein Bild pp. 57, 62, 86; Topham Picturepoint p. 62; Unknown pp. 50, 52, 78, 93, 94.

Written sources
Source D, p. 6 and Source A, p. 87, M. Collier and P. Pedley, *Germany 1919–45*, Heinemann, 2001; Source B, p. 48, Sefton Delmer; Source F, p. 49, S. Waugh, *Essential Modern World History*, Nelson Thornes, 2001; Source F, p. 52, G. Lacey and K. Shephard, *Germany 1918–45*, John Murray, 1971; Source A, p. 55, Nora Waln quoted in *Reaching for the Stars*, Little, Brown & Co., 1939; Source C, p. 55, Stefan Zender; Source D, p. 56, Source F, p.73 and Source I, p. 97, J.A. Cloake, *Germany 1918–45*, Oxford University Press; Source E, p. 56, B. Walsh, *GCSE Modern World*, John Murray, 1996; Source B, p. 65, M. Housden, 'Germans and their opposition to the Third Reich', *History Review 19*, September 1994; Source G, p. 73, J. Hite and C. Hinton, *Weimar and Nazi Germany*, Hodder Murray, 2000, reprinted by permission of John Murray (Publishers) Ltd; Source F, p. 76, Charles Hannam, *A Boy in Your Situation*, Andre Deutsch, 1977; Source G, p. 76, quoted in *Nationalist Socialist Educator*; Source E, p. 78, A. Klonne, *Youth in the Third Reich*, 1982; Source F, p. 79, B. Sax and D. Kuntz, *Inside Hitler's Germany*, Heath & Co., 1992; Source B, p. 87, W. Simpson, *Hitler and Germany*, Cambridge University Press, 1991; Source E, p. 85, Chris Trueman, www.historylearningsite.co.uk/nazis_and_the_german_economy.htm; Source C, p. 95 and Source H, p. 97, quoted in J. Hite and C. Hinton, *Weimar and Nazi Germany*, Hodder Murray, 2000, reprinted by permission of John Murray (Publishers) Ltd; Source E, p. 96, Errikos Sevillias, *From Athens to Auschwitz* (trans. Nikis Stavroulakis), Lycabettus Press, 1983.

Every effort has been made to contact copyright holders of material reproduced in this book. Any omissions will be rectified in subsequent printings if notice is given to the publishers.

Websites
There are links to relevant websites in this book. In order to ensure that the links are up to date, that the links work, and that the sites are not inadvertently linked to sites that could be considered offensive, we have made the links available on the Heinemann website at www.heinemann.co.uk/hotlinks. When you access the site, the express code is 4448P.

Disclaimer
This Edexcel publication offers high-quality support for the delivery of Edexcel qualifications. Edexcel endorsement does not mean that this material is essential to achieve any Edexcel qualification, nor does it mean that this is the only suitable material available to support any Edexcel qualification. No endorsed material will be used verbatim in setting any Edexcel examination and any resource lists produced by Edexcel shall include this and other appropriate texts.

Copies of official specifications for all Edexcel qualifications may be found on the Edexcel website – www.edexcel.com.

Contents

Welcome to this Edexcel GCSE History B: Schools History Project Resource

Option 2C: Life in Germany c1919–c1945

These resources have been written to fully support Edexcel's new GCSE History B: Schools History Project redeveloped specification. This specification has a focus on change and development through studies of societies in depth and of key themes over time. Written by experienced examiners and packed with exam tips and activities, the book includes lots of engaging features to enthuse students and provide the range of support needed to make teaching and learning a success for all ability levels.

Features of this book

- Learning outcomes structure learning at the start of each topic.

- FASCINATING FACTS give learning extra depth.

- Key words are highlighted and defined for easy reference.

- A topic Summary captures the main learning points.

- Activities Activities provide stimulating tasks for the classroom and homework.

How to use this book

Edexcel GCSE History B: Schools History Project Life in Germany c1919–c1945 is divided into three sections that match the specification: The rise of the Nazi Party, the Government of the Third Reich, and the Social impact of the Nazi state.

 A dedicated suite of revision resources for complete exam success. We've broken down the six stages of revision to ensure that you are prepared every step of the way.

 How to get into the perfect 'zone' for your revision.

 Tips and advice on how to effectively plan your revision.

 A checklist of things you should know, revision activities and practice exam questions at the end of each section plus additional exam practice at the end of the book.

 Last-minute advice for just before the exam.

 An overview of what you will have to do in the exam, plus a chance to see what a real exam paper will look like.

 What do you do after your exam? This section contains information on how to get your results and answers to frequently asked questions on what to do next.

ResultsPlus

These features are based on how students have performed in past exams. They are combined with expert advice and guidance from examiners to show you how to achieve better results.

There are five different types of ResultsPlus features throughout this book:

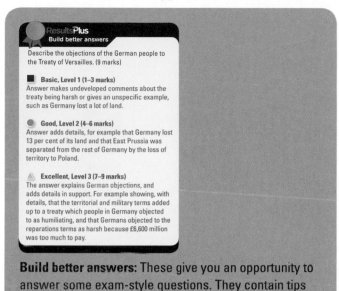

Build better answers: These give you an opportunity to answer some exam-style questions. They contain tips for what a basic ○ good ■ and excellent △ answer will contain.

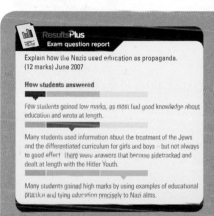

Exam question report: These show previous exam questions with details about how well students answered them.

- Red shows the number of students who scored low marks (less than 35% of the total)
- Orange shows the number of students who did okay (scoring between 35% and 70% of the total marks)
- Green shows the number of students who did well (scoring over 70% of the total marks).

They explain how students could have achieved the top marks so that you can make sure that you answer these questions correctly in future.

Maximise your marks: These are featured in the KnowZone (see below) at the end of each chapter. They include an exam-style question with a student answer, examiner comments and an improved answer so that you can see how to build a better response.

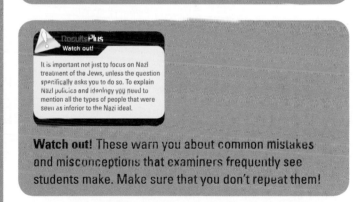

Watch out! These warn you about common mistakes and misconceptions that examiners frequently see students make. Make sure that you don't repeat them!

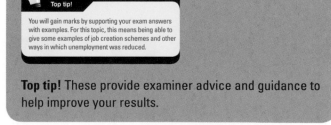

Top tip! These provide examiner advice and guidance to help improve your results.

The rise of the Nazi Party

Introduction

German defeat in the First World War brought about the downfall of the German ruler, Kaiser William II, in 1918. He was replaced by a republic, which was set up in 1919, in the south German town of Weimar.

The Weimar Republic enjoyed mixed fortunes. It was very unpopular in its early years, 1919–1923, mainly because it signed the hated Treaty of Versailles, but also because of hyperinflation. However, it recovered in the years 1923–1929, mainly due to the work of Gustav Stresemann, only to become unpopular again in the years after 1929 as a result of the Great Depression.

The development of the Nazi Party, set up in 1920 by Adolf Hitler, was very much influenced by the fortunes of the Weimar Republic. When the Republic was popular, in the years 1924–1929, the Nazis had little support. However, as the Republic became more and more unpopular after 1929, because of high unemployment, support for Hitler and the Nazis increased.

German children play with bundles of real money.

This cartoon is about the Treaty of Versailles.

Aims and outcomes

By the end of this section, you should be able to understand, explain and describe...

- the fortunes of the Weimar Republic in the years 1919–1932
- the key features of the Nazi Party, 1919–1928
- the reasons for increased support for the Nazi Party in the years 1929–1932

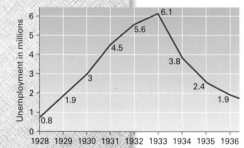

The effects of the Wall Street Crash on unemployment.

1918	1919	1920	1921	1923	1924	1925
Kaiser abdicates and Germany signs the armistice.	Weimar Republic is set up and signs the Treaty of Versailles. Spartacist uprising.	Kapp Putsch and setting up of the Nazi Party.	Hitler becomes leader of the Nazi Party.	French occupation of the Ruhr, hyperinflation and the Munich Putsch.	Hitler spends nine months in prison. The Dawes Plan is signed.	Germany signs the Locarno Treaties.

A 1932 Nazi election poster: 'Women! Millions of men without work. Millions of children without a future. Save the German family. Vote Adolf Hitler!'

Activities

1 Work in pairs, sitting back-to-back:

   a) Describe the Nazi poster on this page to your partner, who will make a sketch based on your description (rather than from what they can recall from the textbook!).

   b) Both of you compare your partner's version of the poster with the original.

   c) How accurate is the sketch compared to the original?

2 Why do you think this poster encouraged German voters to support Hitler and the Nazi Party?

3 What Nazi ideas can you identify from the poster?

FASCINATING FACT
Adolf Hitler, who became ruler of Germany in the 1930s and arguably the most powerful leader in the world, spent several years in his late teens and early twenties as a down-and-out in Vienna.

1926	1928	1929	1930	1932
Germany joins the League of Nations.	Nazis win only twelve seats in the Reichstag.	Death of Stresemann. Wall Street Crash.	Nazis win 105 seats in the Reichstag.	Unemployment reaches 6 million. Nazis win 230 seats and become the largest Party in the Reichstag.

1.1 The early years: the Weimar Republic, 1919–1923

Learning outcomes

By the end of this topic you should be able to:

- understand the early problems of the Weimar Republic
- explain the reasons for early opposition to the Weimar Republic
- describe how successful the Weimar Republic was in dealing with these problems and the opposition it encountered

Activities

Look at the storyboard.

1 What reasons are suggested for the early unpopularity of the Weimar Republic?
2 Which groups wanted to overthrow the Republic?

Getting an overview

In November 1918 there was a revolution in Germany due to defeat in the First World War. Kaiser William II was forced to abdicate and was replaced by a republic.

The Weimar Republic was set up in 1919. The Republic was ruled by a President, a Chancellor and parliament, but it had too many political parties, which led to it being ruled by weak governments.

The Republic was unpopular because it was forced to sign the Treaty of Versailles, which many Germans disagreed with.

There were two attempts to overthrow the Republic in the years 1919–1922. One was by communists known as the Spartacists, and the other by members of the army – in the Kapp Putsch.

Hitler hated the Treaty of Versailles and the new Republic and was determined to destroy them both. He believed that the Republic had betrayed the German army and the German people.

By 1922 Hitler had set up the Nazi Party, which had its own private army, known as the Brownshirts, and its own emblem, the swastika. Hitler wanted to overthrow the Republic by force.

Armistice: Ceasefire

Coalition: A government by two or more political parties

Constitution: System of rules by which a country is governed

Judiciary: Judges

Kaiser: Emperor

Orator: A fluent and effective public speaker

Putsch: An uprising, an attempt to overthrow the government

Reichstag: Parliament

Reparations: Compensation for war damages, paid by a defeated state

Spartacists: The name of the German Communist Party

The formation of the Weimar Republic

Why was there a revolution in Germany in November 1918?

The revolution in November 1918 was due to Germany's defeat in the First World War. Germany had gone to war in 1914 against France, Britain and Russia, confident of an early victory. Although generally successful in the east against Russia, the German armed forces were dragged into a long drawn-out conflict with France and Britain on the Western Front. The entry of the United States in 1917 against Germany tipped the balance of the conflict and by early November 1918 German armies were in retreat, and Germany itself was threatened with occupation.

Furthermore, the war had brought terrible hardships to the German people. The British navy had blockaded the German coastline throughout the war, preventing the import of much-needed supplies of raw materials and food. By 1918 there were serious food shortages and increasing opposition to the war. In addition, a serious flu epidemic killed many German people.

Source A: A cartoon drawn in 1918. The cartoon shows Kaiser William II in the centre with figures on either side, representing war on the left and starvation on the right.

Source B: From a telephone call made by Gustav Noske, one of the leaders of the Social Democrats.

> '... The situation is almost hopeless. General chaos is imminent and power is slipping more and more into the hands of revolutionary sailors.'

The revolution originated from sailors in the German navy in the port of Kiel. At the end of October 1918, they refused to set out to fight the British navy. Instead they marched to Berlin where they were joined by many discontented civilians, all demanding the abdication of **Kaiser** William II, who was blamed for Germany's defeat. On 9 November the Kaiser abdicated and went to live in exile in Holland. On the following day, a republic was set up under its new President, Friedrich Ebert, who was the leader of the Social Democratic Party. Finally, on 11 November, the new republic agreed to an **armistice**.

What was the 'stab in the back' theory?

The 'stab in the back' theory was the belief, put forward by leading members of the German army, and later supported by Hitler and the Nazis, that the German army had been on the verge of winning the war when they were betrayed by the politicians of the new republic, who agreed to the armistice. Although untrue, the theory was believed by many Germans, who refused to accept that Germany had been defeated. This meant that the Republic was unpopular with many from the start.

How was the Weimar Republic set up?

Germany was a federation of eighteen states, each with its own parliament, police and laws. In January 1919, elections took place for a new parliament. This new parliament met in the south German town of Weimar, because of the fighting that was taking place in Berlin between the **Spartacists** and the *Freikorps* (see page 11). The parliament made two important decisions. First of all, it elected Ebert as President. Secondly, it set up a new **constitution** for the new Germany.

Activities

1 What is the message of the cartoonist in Source A?
2 Was this unpopularity justified?

What were the strengths and weaknesses of the new constitution?

The President

Elected every seven years. Had the power to appoint the Chancellor. Article 48 said that in an emergency the president could make laws without going to the Reichstag.

The Chancellor

Appointed by the President and equivalent of the British Prime Minister. Had to have the support of the majority of the Reichstag.

The Reichstag

Equivalent of the House of Commons. Power to pass or reject changes in the law. Elected by proportional representation every four years.

The German people

All adults over the age of twenty could vote for the President and the Reichstag. Had equal rights including the right of free speech, to travel freely, to hold political meetings and freedom of religious belief.

Source C: From a history of Germany 1918–1945, written in 1945.

'The new constitution had many strengths. All Germans had equal rights, including the right to vote. A strong President was necessary to keep control over the government and to protect the country in a crisis. The states had their own traditions and kept their own governments and some control over their own affairs.'

Proportional representation

Proportional representation was one of the strengths of the new constitution, but one of its weaknesses at the same time. Positively, it made sure that all parties were given a fair share of the seats in the **Reichstag** but, on the other hand, it seriously weakened the government of the new republic.

It led to many often small parties, including extremist groups such as the Nazis.

↓

No one party was large enough to secure a majority in the Reichstag.

↓

Several parties often had to join together to form a **coalition** government.

↓

These coalition governments were often weak and short lived.

Source D: The results of the elections of 1920 for the Reichstag.

Party	Percentage of votes	Number of seats
Social Democrats (SPD)	22	102
Centre (Zentrum)	13.6	64
Liberal Progressives (DDP)	8.3	39
Conservatives (DNVP)	15.1	71
Independent Socialists (USP)	19.7	84
National Liberals (DVP)	13.9	65
Communists (KPD)	2.1	4

The constitution had several other weaknesses. The Republic had many enemies and the new constitution gave opposition groups the freedom to criticise and even attack the new government. Moreover, the constitution made no attempt to change traditional institutions, such as the army and **judiciary**, who had supported the Kaiser and did not welcome the new republic. This undermined the Republic from the outset. Additionally, the President had too much power, most especially with the use of Article 48 (see page 35) in a time of emergency.

Activities

3 What does Source D suggest about proportional representation?

4 Working in pairs, make a copy of the following grid to use for your answers. You need to research the strengths to complete the left-hand column, while your partner researches the weaknesses to complete the right-hand column.

'The Weimar constitution had more strengths than weaknesses.' From the evidence, how far do you agree or disagree with this view?

Strengths of constitution	Weaknesses of constitution

Together, look at the conclusion suggested by your research.

Each of you should then decide how much you agree or disagree with this conclusion. Explain why.

What were the main terms of the Treaty of Versailles?

In June 1919, Germany was forced by the victorious countries to sign the Treaty of Versailles.

Territorial terms
- Alsace-Lorraine was returned to France.
- West Posen, Upper Silesia and Posen were given to Poland.
- Eupen Malmedy lost to Belgium.
- Danzig was taken over by the League of Nations as a free city.
- Memel was taken over by the League and eventually given in Lithuania in 1923.
- The Saarland was taken over by the League of Nations for 15 years.
- Germany also lost all of its overseas colonies. They were run by the victorious powers on behalf of the League of Nations.

■ Territory lost by Germany in the Treaty

□ Demilitarised land

TERMS OF TREATY OF VERSAILLES

Reparations
The War Guilt Clause meant that the victorious powers could demand compensation from Germany for the damage caused by the war. This was known as reparations. In 1921 the Reparations Commission fixed the sum at £6,600 million, which had to be paid in annual instalments.

War Guilt
Article 231 of the Treaty said that Germany was to blame for causing the war. This was the term that the Germans most resented. They believed that other countries had caused the war and that Germany went to war in self-defence.

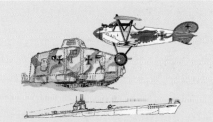

Military terms
- Germany was not allowed military aircraft and no submarines.
- The navy was reduced to six battleships and 15,000 sailors.
- The army was reduced to 100,000.
- The Rhineland area was demilitarised – this meant no German armed forces in the area. Allied troops to occupy the area for fifteen years.

Activities

5 What is meant by the following terms?
   a) Reparations
   b) War Guilt
   c) Demilitarisation of the Rhineland.

6 Study the map of the territorial terms above. Identify two things you can learn from the map about these terms.

7 Which of the four main parts of the Treaty of Versailles punished Germany the most?

In order to look at this, make a copy of the following circle diagram. Then put each of the four main parts of the Treaty in each of the four circles, placing them in order from the worst (from the German point of view) in the centre to the least on the outside circle.

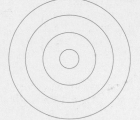

Why was there opposition in Germany to the Versailles Treaty?

Most Germans believed that although they would have to pay a price for losing the war, the terms would be reasonable. After all, their revolution had removed the Kaiser, who had been mainly responsible for the war. He had been replaced by a democratically elected government, which believed that the Allies (Britain, France and the United States) would be sympathetic and not overly harsh. Moreover, the US President, Woodrow Wilson, had promised that it would be a fair treaty based on his 'Fourteen Points'.

The majority of Germans were shocked at the severity of the terms of the Treaty. There was a blaze of protest in the German press and mob violence, especially in Berlin and Hamburg.

The German government had no choice but to accept the terms. Refusal would have precipitated an Allied occupation of Germany. They were, however, blamed by many Germans, most especially Hitler and the Nazis, for the harsh peace terms. The Allies had seriously undermined the position of the new republic.

The German people had many objections to the Treaty. They had not been invited to the peace conference and they described the Treaty as a diktat (or dictated peace), imposed without any opportunity for negotiation or compromise. The military terms threatened to destroy the country's status as a great power and leave Germany vulnerable to attack from neighbours. Possibly more humiliating was the occupation of the Rhineland by Allied troops.

Source E: From a German First World War soldier.

'All of a sudden, we are confronted with what the bulk of the Germans considered an entirely unjust treaty. So resistance against this Treaty was enormous. I think that the strongest resistance concerned the territorial concessions in the East. Nobody was willing to concede that much territory to the new Polish State. Nobody was willing to accept willingly the system of reparations.'

Source F: A cartoon from a German magazine in July 1919. Clemenceau, the French President, is shown as a vampire. The person on the bed represents Germany.

Activities

8 Imagine you are the editor of a German newspaper. Devise a suitable caption for Source F.

9 Why was there strong opposition to the Treaty from many Germans?

Write a brief essay answering this question. You may use the following in your answer together with any other information of your own:

- Reparations
- Military terms
- Territorial terms.

10 Do you agree with the view given in Source G that the 'victors shifted their financial burdens on to the defeated'?

11 Working in pairs, draw a table with two column headings: 'Opposition justified' and 'Opposition not justified'. Complete your table with evidence for each side of the argument.

12 Do you believe that German opposition to the Treaty of Versailles was justified? Explain your conclusion.

The territorial terms seemed to rob Germany of key industrial areas, such as the iron and steel of Alsace-Lorraine and the coalfields of the Saar, as well as raw materials from ex-colonies in Africa and the Far East. The loss of territory to Poland created what became known as the 'Polish Corridor', an area that separated part of Germany, East Prussia, from the rest of Germany. Germany lost 13 per cent of its land.

The War Guilt clause was the one the Germans resented most. To them the war had been one of self-defence. At the very least, from their point of view, other nations such as Russia, France and Britain ought to accept some responsibility for the outbreak of war in 1914. Moreover, Germany had suffered badly as a result of the war and was in no position to make annual **reparation** payments, having lost around 10 per cent of its industry and 15 per cent of its agricultural land.

Source G: The views of John Maynard Keynes.

'The future life of Europe was not the concern of the Allied leaders, its economy was not their anxiety. Their concerns, good and bad alike, related to frontiers and nationalities, to the future weakening of a strong and dangerous enemy, to revenge. The victors shifted their unbearable financial burdens onto the shoulders of the defeated.'

How justified was this opposition?

There has been much discussion and much debate about the Treaty of Versailles, both at the time and later. There were several critics of the Treaty, most notably the famous British economist John Maynard Keynes, who thought that the German opposition to the Treaty was justified. Indeed, he resigned from the British delegation to Versailles in protest at the peace terms. See Source G.

ResultsPlus
Build better answers

Describe the objections of the German people to the Treaty of Versailles. (9 marks)

■ **Basic, Level 1 (1–3 marks)**
Answer makes undeveloped comments about the treaty being harsh or gives an unspecific example, such as Germany lost a lot of land.

● **Good, Level 2 (4–6 marks)**
Answer adds details, for example that Germany lost 13 per cent of its land and that East Prussia was separated from the rest of Germany by the loss of territory to Poland.

▲ **Excellent, Level 3 (7–9 marks)**
The answer explains German objections, and adds details in support. For example showing, with details, that the territorial and military terms added up to a treaty which people in Germany objected to as humiliating, and that Germans objected to the reparations terms as harsh because £6,600 million was too much to pay.

Opposition to the Weimar Republic

The Weimar Republic was not popular with many Germans in the years 1919–1922. This was partly due to weaknesses in the new constitution, being forced to sign the Treaty of Versailles and the 'stab in the back' theory. Moreover, most Germans were not used to democracy and some wanted the return of the Kaiser. The diagram shows the three main groups that threatened the Weimar Republic.

The Spartacist uprising
This was the name of the German Communist party, which was led by Rosa Luxemburg and Karl Liebneckt. They wanted to overthrow the Republic and set up a communist government. Their attempt to seize power in January 1919, was unsuccessful when the Republic called upon the *Freikorps*, volunteer ex servicemen, who shot the two leaders for 'resisting arrest'.

The Kapp Putsch
This was an attempt by the *Freikorps* to overthrow the Weimar Republic in March 1920, led by Dr Kapp, a strong opponent of the Republic and the Treaty of Versailles. The *Freikorps* seized Berlin and forced the government to flee. The putsch was defeated by a workers' general strike.

The Nazis
Hitler believed in the 'stab in the back theory' and strongly opposed the Treaty of Versailles. He was determined to overthrow the Weimar Republic. By 1920 he had his own party, the Nazis, which, within two years, had attracted a number of supporters as well as its own private army, known as the stormtroopers or Brownshirts.

Activities

1 Make a copy of the following table and list three examples of similarities and differences between the Spartacist uprising and the Kapp Putsch. Lightly shade the similarities and leave the differences white. One example has been done for you.

	Spartacist uprising	Kapp Putsch
1	Wanted to overthrow the Weimar Republic	Wanted to overthrow the Weimar Republic
2		
3		

Who were the Spartacists?

The Spartacist League (named after a famous gladiator called Spartacus who led a revolt in ancient Rome) were communists inspired by the success of the communist takeover in Russia in 1917. They did not believe that Ebert and the Social Democrats would serve the interests of the German working people. They were led by Rosa Luxemburg (known as 'Red Rosa'), a brilliant speaker and writer, and Karl Liebneckt.

Source A: A Spartacist poster. The three heads represent militarism, capitalism and the landowners.

Extreme members of the Spartacists staged an uprising in Berlin on 5 January 1919. They seized the headquarters of the government's newspaper and telegraph bureau and tried to organise a general strike. However, it was badly organised and received little support from the people of Berlin.

The day after the uprising, Ebert, with the support of the army leaders, created a volunteer force of 4,000 ex-soldiers known as the *Freikorps* (Free Corps). They were hard men who hated the communists and liked to fight. By 15 January the Spartacists were crushed. Their two leaders were arrested and, during transportation to prison, were shot by two members of the *Freikorps* while apparently 'resisting arrest'. Their murder genuinely shocked President Ebert.

The Spartacists were important for two main reasons:

• Their uprising highlighted the instability of the Weimar Republic. A socialist, left-wing government had been attacked by an even more left-wing group.

• The uprising left the new republic dependent on the support of the army, which had been needed to crush the revolt. In return for this support, the Republic promised not to change the army leadership.

Activities

2 What is the message being put across by the Spartacists in Source A?

3 Describe the ways in which the Spartacists threatened the new republic.

What was the Kapp Putsch?

The *Freikorps* hated the Treaty of Versailles and the Weimar Republic for signing it. When the Treaty came into effect on 1 January 1920, the government began to reduce the size of their army to 100,000. This cut included disbanding the *Freikorps*.

The *Freikorps* were furious and in March 1920, led by Dr Wolfgang Kapp, an extreme nationalist, they attempted to take power in Berlin. Kapp set up a new government in Berlin. The Weimar government fled to Dresden but, before leaving Berlin, called upon the trades unions of Berlin to organise a general strike in order to paralyse the city, cutting off gas, electricity, food and coal supplies and bringing industry to a halt. However, the army refused to move against Kapp and his 5,000 followers.

Nonetheless, Kapp found he could not rule Germany because of the chaos caused by the general strike. He had to abandon his plans and flee to Sweden.

The Kapp **Putsch** showed that the Republic had gained much support from the workers of Berlin. On the other hand, it revealed the lack of support from the army who sympathised with the aims of the Putsch.

Activities

4 Why do you think the army refused to move against Kapp and his followers?

5 Which was the more serious threat to the Republic – the Spartacist uprising or the Kapp Putsch? Give your reasons.

Who was Adolf Hitler?

Munich
In May 1913 Hitler moved to Munich, partly because of the prominence of Jews in Vienna, but mainly to avoid possible arrest for failure to register for military service in the Austrian army between 1909 and 1912.

Birth
Hitler was born in 1889 in the village of Braunau, in Austria. His father, who he disliked, was a customs official and died when Adolf was fourteen. His mother, who he worshipped, died when he was 18.

Education
He spent five years at primary school followed by four years at middle school. He did not do well at school and described his teachers as *'absolute tyrants. They had no sympathy with youth. Their one object was to stuff our brains and turn us into educated apes'*. He left school with no qualifications.

**Adolf Hitler.
This is your life!**

Soldier
When the First World War broke out, Hitler enthusiastically volunteered to serve in the German army. Later he wrote *'I am not ashamed even today to say that, overwhelmed by impassioned enthusiasm, I had fallen on my knees and thanked God'*. He was a good soldier who won medals for bravery. His officers noticed that he was a very effective speaker and gave him the job of countering enemy propaganda.

Vienna
Hitler was determined to be an artist. However, his hopes were dashed when, in 1907, he failed the entrance exam to the Vienna Academy of Fine Arts. He soon ran out of money and was forced to live in a hostel for the homeless, living no better than a down-and-out. He raised some money by painting and selling postcards. It was in Vienna that he first developed his hatred for the Jews as well as his belief in nationalism. In February 1914 he returned to Vienna but was found unfit for the army.

Source B: From Hitler's autobiography *Mein Kampf*, written in 1925.

'I was orphaned at the age of seventeen and was forced to earn my living as a simple worker. I became a labourer on a building site and during the next two years, did every type of casual job. With great effort I was able to teach myself to paint in my spare time. I earned a small living by this work. By the age of 21 I had become an architectural draughtsman and painter and was completely independent.'

Source C: Hitler as a soldier in 1917.

Activities

6   Study Source B. Is this a true account of Hitler's life in Vienna? Why do you think he wrote this account?

7   Make a copy of the following table and complete it with information about Hitler's early life.

Positive achievements	Negative experiences

How did Hitler become the leader of the Nazis?

In 1918 Hitler was badly gassed and was in hospital when the armistice was signed in November 1918. Source C tells how he reacted when he heard of Germany's surrender.

Source D: From *Mein Kampf*.

'It became impossible for me to sit still one minute more. I tottered and groped my way back to my dormitory, threw myself on my bunk, and dug my burning head into my blanket and pillow and sobbed.'

Germany's defeat in 1918 left Hitler extremely bitter and, like many other Germans, he needed a scapegoat, someone to blame for the defeat. In the same way as many other soldiers, he blamed Germany's defeat on the communists and Jews, who he felt had stabbed the German army in the back. After the war, he returned to Munich.

However, he was still employed by the army to check up on any extremist groups in Munich. In September 1919 Hitler was sent to a meeting of a small extremist group known as the German Workers' Party, which had been set up earlier in the year by Anton Drexler. It only had six members. Within a week, he had joined and became committee member number seven. This was partly because he was impressed with the Party's ideas. Drexler wanted to appeal to the working classes but also was a strong nationalist who opposed the Treaty of Versailles. Moreover, Hitler realised he had more chance of becoming leader of a small group rather than one of the bigger, mainstream parties.

In February 1920 he was put in charge of propaganda. He bought control of a newspaper, *The Munich Observer*. On 24 February 1920 he advertised a meeting. Almost 2,000 people attended. At this meeting, Hitler announced the Party's new name: the National Socialist German Workers' Party (NSDAP) or Nazis. He also announced his Twenty-Five Point programme.

Hitler showed a real talent for public speaking and attracted an increasing number of followers to the Party. By 1921 he was strong enough to challenge Drexler and take over the leadership of the Party himself.

Source E: A photograph of Nazi supporters in Bavaria, 1920. Hitler is second from the left.

Source F: Karl Luedecke, one of Hitler's earliest supporters, describing an early meeting of the newly formed Nazi Party.

'When he spoke of Germany's disgrace, I felt ready to spring at an enemy. His appeal to the honour of German manhood was like a call to arms, and the gospel he preached a sacred revelation… I forgot everything but this man. When I looked around, I saw that his power of suggestion was magnetising those as one. I had an experience which was comparable to a religious conviction.'

Activities

8 What can you learn from Source F about Hitler's qualities as a speaker?

9 Explain how Hitler had managed to become leader of the Nazi Party by 1921.

What were the main features of the early Nazi Party, 1920–1922?

The Nazi Party was based in Munich but it soon began to spread to other parts of Germany. The Nazis published their own newspapers to spread their ideas and received support from extreme nationalists and anti-communists. By 1922 the Nazi Party had 6,000 members, rising to 50,000 two years later.

The swastika

Hitler himself designed the Nazi flag with the swastika symbol. The three colours, red, white and black, had been the colours of the German flag under the Kaiser. Red represented the socialist part of the Party, the white the nationalist and the swastika itself Hitler's racial views.

Hitler

Hitler's personal qualities, especially as an **orator**, encouraged many to join the Nazi Party. He put great faith in the spoken word, and stage-managed and rehearsed his speeches carefully. He would use a long and gradual build-up to increase the anticipation of the audience. He practised his gestures and studied photographs of himself in action. The SA, Hitler's personal bodyguard, were there to deal with hecklers.

Source G: A supporter describes a Nazi meeting in 1926.

'A storm of jubilation rising from afar, from the street and moving into the lobby, announced the coming of the Fuhrer. And then suddenly the auditorium went wild, as he strode resolutely in his raincoat and without a hat to the rostrum. When the speech came to an end I could not see out of my eyes any more. There were tears in my eyes, my throat was all tight from crying… I looked round discreetly, and noticed that others, too, men and women and young fellows were as deeply affected as I.'

Source H: A painting of Hitler speaking to a Nazi Party meeting in 1921.

The SA

In 1921 Hitler set up the *Sturm Abteilung* (SA) (also known as the stormtroopers). It attracted many ex-soldiers, especially from the *Freikorps*. These were men who felt betrayed by the Treaty of Versailles. The SA would disrupt the meetings of Hitler's opponents, especially the communists, and often beat up opposition supporters. They were also known as the 'Brownshirts' because of the colour of their uniform. Ernst Röhm, one of the founder members of the German Workers' Party in 1919, became the leader of the SA.

The Party programme

The Nazi Party programme was kept vague and deliberately designed to appeal to as many groups as possible:

- Nationalism appealed with the promise to destroy the Treaty of Versailles and introduce rearmament.
- Socialism appealed to the workers. The Nazis promised to give workers a share in company profits, to nationalise big companies, and to share out land for the benefit of everyone.
- Anti-Semitism or hatred of the Jews appealed to those Germans who needed a scapegoat for Germany's defeat in the First World War and also those who were resentful of Jewish wealth.

- Hitler hated communism and promised to remove the threat from the German Communist Party. This appealed to the middle classes and big business: both of these groups would lose out if the communists took over the German government.

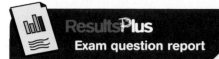

ResultsPlus
Exam question report

How far were the problems faced by the Weimar Republic in the years 1919 to 1923 caused by the Treaty of Versailles? Explain your answer.

How students answered

Those that scored poorly for this question could describe the Treaty in some detail. However, this was not linked to the events in the period. Some candidates did not focus on the period of the question and instead referred to the Wall Street Crash and/or Stresemann.

Better answers could explain the events and problems of the Republic and relate them to the Treaty of Versailles.

The best answers assessed the problems of the period against the Treaty and the actions of the government, for example, the terms of the Treaty led to economic problems but the behaviour of the Weimar Republic made the situation worse. There were some excellent uses of the terms of the Treaty to explain the uprisings against the government.

Activities

10 'Hitler was the main reason for increasing membership of and support for the Nazi Party in the years 1920–1922.' Working in pairs answer the following:

   a) What evidence is there to support this view?

   b) What other features of the Nazi Party would attract increasing membership and support?

   c) What other developments in Weimar Germany, 1919–1921, would favour the Nazi Party?

   d) What is your final conclusion about this view?

11 'The Weimar Republic was doomed to failure from the very start.' Discuss.

Summary

- The Weimar Republic was set up after the revolution of November 1918. It introduced a new constitution, which had several weaknesses, especially the use of proportional representation, which encouraged weak coalition governments.

- The new republic got off to a bad start because it had to sign the Treaty of Versailles. This Treaty was unpopular with many Germans because of its harsh terms, especially the War Guilt clause and the payment of reparations.

- The Weimar Republic survived two attempts to overthrow it, one from the left and one from the right: the Spartacist uprising of January 1919 and the Kapp Putsch of March 1920.

- In 1921 Hitler became leader of the Nazi Party, which by 1921 had its own private army, the SA, and was preparing for an armed uprising.

15

1918
Abdication of Kaiser William II

Armistice

1919
Hitler joins German Workers' Party

Spartacist uprising

Treaty of Versailles

1920
Kapp Putsch

German Workers' Party renamed Nazi Party

1921
Hitler becomes leader of the Nazi Party

1.2 Challenges and recovery: the impact of economic problems, 1923–1929

Learning outcomes

By the end of this topic you should be able to:

- understand the causes and effects of the hyperinflation of 1923
- explain the importance of the Munich Putsch of 1923
- describe how far the Weimar Republic recovered in the years 1924–1929

Hyperinflation: When prices go up very quickly

Passive resistance: To resist authority in a peaceful, non-violent way

The Ruhr: The industrial part of Germany producing coal, iron and steel

Source A: Women and children on a coal tip in Germany in 1923.

Getting an overview

French troops seize the Ruhr

In January 1923 French troops occupied the Ruhr industrial area of Germany because the German government was unable to make its first reparations payment. The Weimar Republic was power-less to do anything although German workers in the Ruhr used passive resistance by refusing to work for the French and factories came to a standstill.

Revolution in a Beer Hall

In November 1923 Hitler and the SA raided a Beer Hall in Munich and captured two of the leaders of Bavaria. They hoped to persuade them to support a Nazi takeover. The leaders escaped and the revolution was defeated. Hitler was arrested and put on trial. He was sentenced to five years in prison but only served nine months during which he wrote his autobiography, *Mein Kampf.*

The mark is worthless

By November 1923 Germany was suffering from hyperinfla-tion. The German mark became worthless and it cost one and half million marks for a loaf of bread. Many people lost all of their savings whilst workers and pensioners were unable to buy everyday necessities. The Weimar Republic became more unpopular than ever.

Germany recovers under Stresemann

Germany recovered from the disasters of 1923 mainly due to the leadership of the Foreign Secretary, Gustav Stresemann. He reduced inflation by introducing the Rentenmark. He also reduced reparation payments through the Dawes and Young Plans and encouraged the USA to make loans to German industry. Germany was allowed to join the League of Nations and, once again, became an important power.

Activities

1. Study Source A. What are the women and children doing in this photograph?
2. What impression does the photograph give about Germany in 1923?
3. Match the following alternative headlines to the newspaper cuttings shown in the overview above:
   - The USA rescues Germany
   - Prices rocket out of control
   - Workers refuse to co-operate with invaders
   - Munich fiasco.

The causes and effects of hyperinflation

Why did French troops occupy the Ruhr in 1923?

The German government had been unable to make its first reparations payment in 1922. Instead, it requested extra time for the payment, but France refused. Therefore, in January 1923, the French marched into **the Ruhr** industrial area of Germany, determined to get payment in kind for the money owed.

Source A: A French magazine cover showing French soldiers in the Ruhr in January 1923. The caption at the foot reads: 'At the gates of every public building and factory, the blue helmets of our soldiers remind the forgetful Germans of France's rightful claims.'

Le Petit Journal
illustré

'12 Pages   12 Pages
HEBDOMADAIRE
61, rue Lafayette, Paris   PRIX : 0 fr. 30
28 Janvier 1923

Pour que l'Allemagne paie
L'occupation de la région industrielle de la Ruhr s'est faite sans coup férir. Aux portes de tous les monuments publics et de toutes les usines, les capotes bleues de nos soldats rappellent aux Allemands oublieux les légitimes revendications et la ferme volonté de la France.

How did Germany react to the occupation?

The German government was unable to offer any armed resistance. Instead, the workers chose **passive resistance** and went on strike, refusing to work for the foreign army of occupation. Some even took more direct action. They set some of the factories on fire and sabotaged the pumps in some mines so they flooded and could not be worked. There were clashes with the French troops and a number of strikers were shot.

Source B: An official French army account of the occupation.

'Passive resistance meant not co-operating at all with the French and Belgians. It meant refusing all their demands and orders. The post, the telegraph and telephone workers would have nothing to do with the French and Belgians, to send their letters, to sell them stamps, and so on. Railway workers refused to run the trains needed for the troops.'

What were the effects of the invasion?

The invasion had mixed effects. It united the German people against the French invaders, with the strikers being seen as heroes of the German people. The popularity of the Weimar temporarily increased because it had backed the strikers and organised passive resistance. Nevertheless, it had disastrous effects on the German economy. The government had to print more money to pay the strikers, which in turn increased inflation. The strike meant fewer goods were produced and this made inflation even worse.

Activities

1 Study Source A. Imagine this was to be published in a German magazine. Devise an alternative caption.

2 Do you agree that the French were justified in occupying the Ruhr?

3 'A political success but an economic disaster.' How far do you agree with this view of the effects of the French occupation of the Ruhr on Germany?

What was the impact of the hyperinflation of 1923 on Germany?

What is hyperinflation?

When a government prints too much paper money it then loses value very quickly causing rapid rises in prices. **Hyperinflation** is when prices go up ten, a hundred times or even more in a short space of time.

Why did it happen?

The Weimar government was short of money after the First World War and began to print more and more banknotes. The situation was worsened when the German government was unable to make its first reparations payment in 1922. French troops occupied the Ruhr and the German government was forced to print even more notes. By November 1923 the German mark was worthless.

Activities

4 What is meant by hyperinflation?

5 Identify two things you can learn from Source D about the hyperinflation of 1923.

6 Working in pairs, organise the effects of hyperinflation (in the artwork below) into:
- those who gained
- those who lost.

Source D: Children stacking up German banknotes. Hyperinflation had made real banknotes almost worthless.

What effects did hyperinflation have?

Pensioners found that their pensions became worthless.

People with savings found that they lost all value.

Farmers were pleased when the price of food went up.

Wages could not keep up with the rate of inflation and many people could not afford necessities such as bread.

BREAD ←

Some people did benefit – especially businessmen who had loans which they could now pay off.

What caused hyperinflation?

When a government prints money, the money's value is supported by the amount of gold reserves the government has. For example, if a government has gold reserves to the value of £1 million then it should only print £1 million worth of notes. If it prints £2 million in bank notes, then the notes are only worth half their face value, and so they lose value. In other words, when a government prints money for which it does not have gold supplies, the value of the money goes down and prices go up.

> **First World War**
>
> In 1914 – 4 marks to the dollar
>
> Government began to print more money to pay for the war
>
> In 1919 – 9 marks to the dollar

> **Weimar Government 1919–1922**
>
> Weimar governments faced with shortages and having to pay reparations decided to print more money
>
> January 1921 – 65 marks to the dollar
>
> July 1922 – 493 marks to the dollar

> **French occupation of the Ruhr**
>
> The German government was unable to make its reparation payments in 1922. France and Belgium retaliated, in January 1923, by sending soldiers to occupy the Ruhr industrial area of Germany and taking payment in coal and iron and steel. The German workers decided on passive resistance
>
> January 1923 – 17,972 marks to the dollar

> **Passive resistance**
>
> This meant that the government lost money from the production of coal and iron and steel. It also had to pay the striking Ruhr workers. It printed even more money
>
> November 1923 – 4.2 billion marks to the dollar

Activities

7 Do you agree that the French occupation of the Ruhr was the most important cause of hyperinflation? Explain your reasons.

What were the effects of hyperinflation?

Many Germans actually benefited from hyperinflation. For example, some people with mortgages were able to pay them off. Foreigners in Germany suddenly found that they could exchange dollars or pounds for millions of marks and could afford things that ordinary Germans could not. People who rented property with long-term rents gained as the real value of their payments fell. Exporters gained from the mark's falling exchange rate because their goods, in effect, became cheaper for the customers they were exporting to.

Entrepreneurs with access to cheap credit used loans to extend their holdings. They then easily repaid these loans when their income had increased in money terms.

Source E: A popular joke in 1923.

> 'Two women were carrying a laundry basket filled to the brim with banknotes. Seeing a crowd standing round a shop window, they put down the basket for a moment to see if there was anything they could buy. When they turned round a few moments later, they found the money there untouched. But the basket was gone.'

ResultsPlus
Top tip!

The best answers to questions about hyperinflation mention the different effects on different people – the winners and losers. Not everyone was badly affected and it is important to remember this.

Massive price rises

Wages could not keep up with price rises.

This table shows what happened to the price of bread in Berlin (prices in marks):

July 1923	3,465
August 1923	69,000
September 1923	1,512,000
October 1923	1,743,000,000
November 1923	201,000,000,000

German money became worthless

Some people had been saving for years. These savings became worthless.

Businessmen

Many businessmen who had borrowed money from the banks were able to wipe out their debts. Others were able to take over smaller businesses that were going bankrupt.

Fixed incomes

People on fixed incomes, such as pensions, found that they became worthless.

Farmers

Farmers benefited from the rise in prices of food at a time when the farming industry was not doing well.

Effects of hyperinflation

Workers

Those in employment were generally secure because wages went higher and higher. However, wage rises always lagged behind price rises.

The rich

They usually had land and possessions and were protected from the worst effects of hyperinflation.

The middle class

Many lost faith in the Weimar Republic and were convinced that it was unable to deal with serious economic problems.

Activities

8   In groups of three, prepare a role-play about the effects of hyperinflation on three different people in Germany in November 1923:

 • These could include a businessman, farmer, pensioner, worker, housewife, a foreigner living in Germany, an exporter, an entrepreneur

 • What would be their attitude to the Weimar government?

9   In pairs, draw a balance sheet of the effects of hyperinflation on German people.

The Weimar government had three options in dealing with inflation:

 • raise taxes
 • borrow more money
 • print more money.

Activities

10   In groups, prepare arguments for and against the three options facing the Weimar government during and after the First World War – raise taxes, borrow money or print money.

11   To what extent was printing money the least of the three evils?

12   'The hyperinflation of 1923 was a disaster for all Germans.' Discuss.

Why did Hitler carry out the Munich Putsch?

Hitler's aims

He was determined to overthrow the Weimar Republic by organising a successful revolution in Bavaria and then, with his supporters, organising a march on Berlin.

Influence of Mussolini

The Italian leader, Benito Mussolini, had successfully marched on Rome the previous year and taken over the Italian government.

Bavarian leaders

The Bavarian government was right wing. Its leaders, Gustav von Kahr and General von Lossow, had been plotting against the Weimar Republic. Hitler was convinced that they would support a putsch.

Discontent in Germany

The timing seemed ideal for an armed uprising. The Weimar Republic was more unpopular than ever due to the terrible effects of hyperinflation. Moreover, many nationalists were incensed when, in September 1923, Stresemann's government called off passive resistance in the Ruhr and resumed paying reparations to the French.

Reasons for the Munich Putsch

The Nazi Party

The Nazi Party appeared ready to seize power by force. Hitler was the established leader, it had 50,000 supporters and its own private army, the SA. In addition, Hitler had developed an increasingly close relationship with the former army leader, General Ludendorff. Hitler believed that Ludendorff would be able to persuade the German army to desert the government and side with the Nazis.

Source A: A Bavarian police report, written in September 1923.

'As a result of rising prices and increasing unemployment, the workers are bitter. The patriotic bands are at fever pitch because of the abandonment of the Ruhr resistance.'

Source B: A report by the Munich city council in October 1923.

'In all of Munich (including the food market) absolutely no potatoes have been available for days which, in view of the fact that potatoes are naturally the cheapest food, is particularly tragic at this time.'

Source C: A column of the SA arriving in Munich just before the uprising.

Activities

1 Why would the reports written in Sources A and B have encouraged Hitler to carry out the uprising?

2 How did the following people encourage Hitler to carry out the uprising?

   a) Mussolini

   b) Ludendorff

   c) Gustav von Kahr.

What happened during and after the uprising?

8 November 1923

A large meeting being addressed by Gustav von Kahr, the head of the Bavarian government, in a beer hall in Munich, was suddenly interrupted by Hitler and the SA. They burst into the hall. Hitler jumped on to a table and fired two shots at the ceiling. He announced that he was taking over the government of Bavaria and tried to persuade everyone there to support him. Kahr was locked in a room, from which he managed to escape sometime during the night.

Source D: An eyewitness description.

'Hitler climbed onto a chair to my left. The hall was still restless. Hitler made a sign to the man on his right, who fired a shot at the ceiling. Thereupon Hitler called out: "The national revolution has broken out. The hall is surrounded." He asked Kahr and the other two gentlemen to come out of the room nearby. He guaranteed their personal freedom… Throughout this time, Hitler was radiant with joy. One had the feeling that he was delighted to have succeeded in persuading Kahr to work with him. I would say he had a childlike joy, which I will never forget. By comparison, Ludendorff looked extremely grave and pale. He had the appearance of a man who knew it was a matter of life or death.'

9 November 1923

Hitler and Ludendorff with about 3,000 supporters, some of whom were members of the SA, decided to march through Munich, hoping to win mass public support. As they neared the city centre, armed police blocked their way. The police used rubber truncheons and rifle butts to force back the crowd.

One Nazi shouted 'Don't shoot, Ludendorff and Hitler are coming.'

Hitler cried out 'Surrender!'

Suddenly a shot was heard, but no one knows who fired first. This was followed by a gun battle between the marchers and the police. Hitler fell to the ground. He may have been pushed or simply have tripped over, but he dislocated his shoulder. Although the gun battle only lasted one minute, 16 of the marchers were killed when the police opened fire. Hitler, who had moved to the back of the marchers, apparently lost his nerve and escaped the scene in a motor car. Ludendorff, on the other hand, marched to the next square where he was arrested.

11 November 1923

Hitler was arrested for his part in the uprising.

February 1924

Hitler was put on trial for his part in the uprising, with Kahr appearing as one of the prosecution witnesses. The charge was high treason. However, Hitler turned his trial into a propaganda success, using it to attack the Weimar Republic, whom he accused of treason because of the armistice and the signing of the Treaty of Versailles. The trial provided Hitler with nationwide publicity.

Hitler had made a name for himself. Newspapers throughout Germany and all over the world reported his speech, especially his view that he had organised the uprising to overthrow a Republic that had betrayed the German people. The trial established Hitler as a national leader of opposition to the Weimar Republic. Moreover, the court was sympathetic to Hitler. Instead of sentencing him to death as it might have done, it gave him the minimum sentence for the offence – five years. Ludendorff was let off without a prison sentence. Other Nazi leaders, such as Röhm, the leader of the SA, were given short prison sentences. However, the Nazi Party was banned as a result of the putsch.

February–July 1924: Imprisonment

Hitler only served nine months of his five-year sentence. He was imprisoned in Landsberg Prison but with special conditions. He had his own private room. He was allowed as many visitors as he wished. He spent most of his time dictating his autobiography *Mein Kampf (My Struggle)*, to Rudolf Hess, a leading Nazi. The autobiography not only gave Hitler's version of his life so far, but also

Source E: A painting made later by one of Hitler's followers who took part in the Munich Putsch. In the foreground the police are opening fire on the Nazis. Hitler stands with his arm raised with Ludendorff on his right.

clearly set out his aims for the Nazi Party and how he hoped and expected to achieve power. The main points were the removal of Jews from Germany, the destruction of communism, and the expansion of Germany to the east in order to create more living space, which was called *Lebensraum*.

Source F: From Hitler's evidence at his trial (following the Munich Putsch), February 1924.

'I alone bear responsibility for the putsch but I am not a criminal because of that. There is no such thing as high treason among the traitors of 1918. I only wanted what's best for the German people. I only wanted to lead Germany back to honour, to its proper position in the world. I only wish I had suffered the same fate as my dear slaughtered colleagues.'

Activities

3 Does the painting shown in Source E give an accurate view of the events of the Munich uprising? Explain your answer.

4 Suggest two reasons for the failure of the uprising.

5 Why was Hitler given such a short prison sentence?

Was the uprising a failure?

The uprising appeared to have been a disastrous and humiliating failure. Hitler had failed to win the support of Kahr, the Bavarian army and the police. He had run away from the gun battle of 9 November, but then been arrested. He was found guilty at his trial and spent nine months in prison.

However, there were some positive consequences for Hitler and the Nazi Party, more especially from his trial.

Source G: A photograph showing Hitler and Ludendorff outside the Munich courtroom.

Hitler also made use of his trial to attack the Weimar Republic and ensure maximum publicity for himself throughout Germany. In addition, the failure prompted Hitler to rethink his tactics, realising that a future armed uprising would be doomed to failure.

Source H: Hitler speaking in the mid 1920s.

'Instead of working to achieve power by an armed coup, we shall have to hold our noses and enter the Reichstag against the opposition deputies. If outvoting them takes longer than outshooting them, at least the results will be guaranteed by their own constitution. Sooner or later we shall have a majority and after that – Germany.'

Hitler himself believed that the failure was a blessing in disguise.

Source I: From a speech by Hitler in 1933.

'It was the greatest good fortune for us Nazis that the putsch collapsed because:

1   The sudden takeover of power in the whole of Germany would have led to the greatest difficulties in 1923 because the essential preparations had not even been begun by the Nationalist Socialist Party.

2   Most important of all, the bloody sacrifice of 9 November 1923 has proven the most effective propaganda for National Socialism.'

Activities

6   Copy the ideas map below to show the consequences of the Munich Putsch. Highlight what you believe to be the most important consequence and explain your choice.

```
              ┌──────────────┐
              │              │
              └──────────────┘
                     ↑
┌────────┐    ┌─────────────────┐    ┌────────┐
│        │ ←  │  Consequences of │  → │        │
└────────┘    │  the Munich Putsch│    └────────┘
              └─────────────────┘
                  ↙        ↘
        ┌────────┐        ┌────────┐
        │        │        │        │
        └────────┘        └────────┘
```

7   Study Source I. Do you agree with the views expressed by Hitler? Explain your answer.

8   Do you agree that Hitler was able to turn defeat at Munich into victory?

The recovery of the Republic, 1924–1929

During the years 1924 to 1929 the Weimar Republic appeared to recover from the disasters of 1923.

Reasons for recovery	Evidence of recovery
The recovery was due to several factors: • Gustav Stresemann, who was Foreign Secretary, played a leading role, especially in sorting out reparations and hyperinflation • The Dawes Plan of 1924 reduced Germany's reparations • US loans to Germany • The Young Plan of 1929 further reduced reparations payments, which were to be paid over a period of 58 years • Stresemann introduced a new currency called the rentenmark, which ended hyperinflation • In 1925 Germany signed the Locarno Treaties, which guaranteed the frontiers with Belgium, France and Italy • In 1926 Germany was allowed to join the League of Nations	• There was little support for extremist parties such as the Nazis, who only won twelve seats in the elections of 1928 • There was more support for parties such as the Social Democrats, who supported the Republic • Germany was accepted again as an important power in Europe • New factories were built • There was a fall in unemployment • New roads and railways were built, as well as nearly 3 million new homes • Prosperity was shown by new airships, ocean liners, radio stations and film studios • Foreign banks, especially in the US, lent nearly 25,000 billion marks to German borrowers

Source A: 1920s Berlin.

Activities

1 Look at Source A. Make a list of evidence of prosperity in Germany in the 1920s.

2 Draw two spider diagrams:

a) one showing reasons for recovery

b) the other giving examples of recovery.

What was the role of Stresemann?

There has been much debate about why Germany recovered in the years 1924–1929, especially concerning the importance of the part played by Gustav Stresemann. He was a very good speaker and administrator and, in August 1923, was appointed Chancellor in order to deal with the problems of hyperinflation. It was his decision to call off passive resistance in the Ruhr. However, by November 1923, he had lost the support of the Reichstag as Chancellor. Instead, he became Foreign Secretary until his death in October 1929.

Stresemann followed a policy of fulfilment: this meant co-operating with France and Britain in order to remove or reduce some of the terms of the Treaty of Versailles, especially reparations. He outlined his aims in a letter to the son of the former Kaiser William II, in September 1925.

Source B: From Stresemann's letter to the former Kaiser's son.

'In my opinion there are three great tasks that confront German foreign policy in the immediate future:

1 The solution of the reparations problem in a way that is tolerable for Germany.

2 The protection of those ten to twelve million Germans who now live under foreign control in foreign lands.

3 The readjustment of our eastern frontiers; the recovery of Danzig, the Polish Corridor, and a correction of the frontier in Upper Silesia.'

He was responsible for a number of measures, including the introduction of the Dawes Plan, to deal with Germany's problems. The hyperinflation of 1923 had destroyed the value of the German mark. In order to stabilise the currency, Stresemann introduced a temporary currency called the Rentenmark in November 1923. This was issued in limited numbers, and had its value based not on gold reserves but on a mortgage of Germany's entire industrial and agricultural resources. In other words, a Rentenmark could, in theory, be exchanged for a piece of land or industry. This did not happen, because the German people showed confidence in the new currency. In the following year, the Rentenmark was converted into the Reichsmark, another new currency, now backed with gold. This measure gradually restored the value of the mark, stabilised the German financial system and greatly reduced inflation.

Stresemann greatly improved relations with Britain and France by ending passive resistance in the Ruhr and signing the Locarno Treaties of 1925. These Treaties also included Italy and guaranteed Germany's frontiers with France, Belgium and Italy. The period 1925–1929 became known as the 'Locarno Honeymoon' and furthered Stresemann's policy of fulfilment, co-operation abroad to reduce reparations and further German economic recovery. Indeed, in 1926 Stresemann was awarded the Nobel Peace Prize.

Source C: A poster urging voters to reject the Young Plan. It says: 'You must slave into the third generation.'

In the following year, Stresemann took Germany into the League of Nations. Germany was recognised as a great power and given a permanent seat on the League's council alongside France and Britain.

In 1928, Germany signed the Kellogg-Briand Pact along with 64 other nations. It was agreed that they would keep their armies for self-defence but would solve all future disputes by 'peaceful means'. Peace would further assist German economic recovery and growth.

What other reasons were there for recovery?

There were other reasons for German economic recovery, especially the Dawes and Young Plans and loans from the United States.

The Dawes Plan of 1924, negotiated between the USA and Germany, but with the support of France and Britain, reorganised Germany's reparation payments. These were not only reduced but were also more sensibly staged to match Germany's capacity to pay. For the first five years, German payments would start at £50 million, increasing to £150 million over the five-year period. Thereafter, the payments would be linked to Germany's capacity to pay. In return, the French withdrew their troops from the Ruhr.

Furthermore, the Dawes Plan included a US loan of 800 million gold marks to Germany. Over the following six years, Germany borrowed about $3,000 million from US banks. This greatly assisted the growth of German industry as well as the payment of reparations. German nationalists opposed the Dawes Plan, which they described as 'a second Versailles'. They resented the Dawes Plan because it gave the Allies partial control over Germany's railways and the German state bank. Moreover, it was an admission that Germany had caused the war, which they totally disagreed with.

In 1929, Germany negotiated a further change to reparations, known as the Young Plan. For the first time a timescale for reparations repayments was set, with Germany making repayments for the next 59 years until 1988. The repayments were fixed at 2,000 million marks a year (reduced from the 2,500 million marks set by the Dawes Plan). In addition, responsibility for repayment was given to Germany, rather than the Allies. In return for this agreement, the French promised to evacuate the Rhineland by June 1930, five years ahead of schedule.

However, there was strong opposition to the Young Plan from nationalist groups, who were against any further payments of reparations, especially staged over so many years. Alfred Hugenberg, a media tycoon, supported by Hitler and the Nazis, formed the Reich Committee for a Referendum to oppose the Young Plan and raised a petition with 4 million signatures. A referendum was held in December 1929 and resulted in defeat for those who opposed the Young Plan with only 5.8 million or 14 per cent voting to reject it.

Activities

3   In pairs, study Source C.
    a) What is the message of the poster?
    b) What arguments would the supporters of the Young Plan make in reply to this poster?

4   Explain the importance of Stresemann's role in the recovery of the Republic in the years 1924 to 1929.

5   What was the most important reason for German recovery, 1924–1929?

    Make a copy of the following table. Complete the table indicating the level of importance of each person or agreement, giving a brief explanation in the right-hand column.

	Quite important	Important	Very important	Decisive	Reason
Stresemann					
Dawes Plan					
Young Plan					
US loans					

1.3 Increasing support for the Nazi Party, 1925–1932

Learning outcomes

By the end of this topic you should be able to:

● understand which groups supported the Nazi Party in the years 1921–1928

● explain why there was greater support for the Nazis in the years 1929–1932

● describe which groups supported the Nazis in the years 1929–1932

Propaganda: False or misleading information given out to spread certain points of view

Wall Street Crash: Wall Street is the name of the New York stock exchange. Share prices fell disastrously on Wall Street in October 1929

Getting an overview

1924

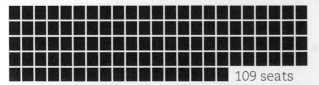

32 seats

The Nazi Party did quite well in the first election they contested for the Reichstag. This was at least partly because of the publicity provided by Hitler's trial. Many Germans were still unhappy about the events of 1923, especially hyperinflation. Hitler began to reorganise the Nazi Party ready to fight future general elections. The main support came from middle-class people who were frightened of communism.

1928

12 seats

The election results of 1928 proved disappointing for the Nazis, but were not surprising. This was the period of recovery under Stresemann, with few voters prepared to support extreme parties such as the Nazis or communists.

1930

109 seats

Within two years the Nazis had become the second largest party in the Reichstag. This was due to the disastrous effects of the Wall Street Crash on Germany. It led to a terrible depression in German industry, with unemployment reaching 4 million by 1930. Many of Hitler's supporters were from the middle classes, who feared a communist takeover.

1932

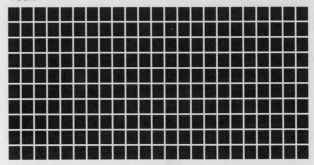

230 seats

In July 1932 the Nazis became the largest party in the Reichstag. Increased support was again due to the effects of the depression, with unemployment peaking at 6 million. The Nazis skilfully exploited the depression by using both clever propaganda (organised by Joseph Goebbels) and the personal appeal of Hitler himself to win over as many groups as possible. The organisation and discipline of the SA impressed many Germans. The Nazis also attracted support from big businesses, the middle classes and some of the unemployed.

Source A: People cutting up the carcass of a horse in a street in Berlin in 1931.

Activities

1 Draw a bar chart to show the seats won by the Nazis in 1924, 1928, 1930 and 1932.

2 For each year, give one reason for the Nazi result.

3 What does Source A suggest about the lifestyle of German people in 1931?

ResultsPlus
Build better answers

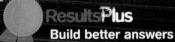

Give two things that you can learn from Source A about the effects of the depression in Germany. (4 marks)

■ **Basic, Level 1 (1–2 marks)**
Answer makes an inference but does not use the source to support it, for example: people were hungry, or people were out of work.

● **Good, Level 2 (3–4 marks)**
Answer uses the source to support the inference. For example, the source suggests that they were desperate for food, otherwise they would not be cutting the horse up. If people were so very hungry, it suggests they were out of work and had no money for food.

How was the Nazi Party reorganised in the years 1924–1928?

The Nazi Party had been banned after the Munich Putsch, but in February 1925 the ban was lifted and Hitler relaunched the Party. It was totally reorganised into a party that could appeal to the electors and win seats in the Reichstag. He also turned it into a national party that was active throughout Germany, not just Bavaria.

Activities

1 Study Source A on the opposite page. What is the message of this poster?

2 Explain why Hitler was able to strengthen the Nazi Party in the years 1924–1928. You may use the following in your answer and any other information of your own.
- Change of tactics
- Goebbels
- Nazi organisations.

Bamberg Conference
Hitler survived threats to his leadership of the Party from Gregor Strasser and Joseph Goebbels. They wanted the Party to become more socialist in order to appeal to the working classes. Hitler was opposed to this and called a Party conference in Bamberg in Bavaria in 1926. His leadership was confirmed and Goebbels became one of his closest supporters.

The SA
This was strengthened with more young men encouraged to join. The image of the organisation was changed, placing the emphasis on discipline and order rather than violence and intimidation.

Nazi organisations
These were set up to appeal to certain interest groups, including the Nazi Students' League, the Teachers' League and the Women's League. The Nazi youth movement was organised to appeal to the young.

Agricultural areas
From 1928, the Nazis focused much more on winning support in agricultural areas. This was because of the depression, which had affected farming throughout the 1920s and worsened in 1927 with a further slump in food prices.

Party rallies
In 1926 a Nazi Party rally was held at Weimar. This began the pattern of military-style parades.

Mein Kampf
Hitler's book, *Mein Kampf*, was published in 1925 and, because of the publicity from Hitler's trial, it became a best seller.

Party organisation
Hitler reorganised the Party to make it more efficient and to ensure it was prepared, even at street level, to fight future elections. He created a national headquarters in Munich and insisted on the central control of finance and membership. Branches of the Party, known as *Gaus*, were set up all over Germany and were placed under the control of a Party official known as a *Gauleiter*.

Propaganda
Goebbels organised Party **propaganda** and used posters skilfully. He also used Nazi newspapers and meetings to put across the Nazi ideals. He discovered that their anti-Jewish message had most appeal among the working classes and increased anti-Semitic propaganda. The Nazis were the only party to run evening classes to train their members in public-speaking skills.

Source A: A Nazi election poster of 1924. The poster shows a figure representing Germany with a Jewish banker on his shoulders.

Who were the Nazi Party's early supporters?

The Nazi Party appears to have attracted support from the following main groups:

- A high proportion of younger members who were either ex-soldiers or were too young to have fought in the First World War greatly admired Hitler. Some of these were university students.
- Middle-class groups such as master craftsmen, clerks and merchants, who lost out in 1923 due to hyperinflation and felt threatened by communism.
- Farmers who were badly affected by the fall in food prices of the 1920s and the onset of a depression in agriculture from 1927.
- Skilled workers such as plumbers and electricians.

Although membership of the Party increased to over 100,000 by 1928, the Nazis did not do well in the Reichstag elections. Having won 32 seats in May 1924, four years later this fell to 12 seats. This was due to the revival of the Republic under Stresemann.

Source B: William Shirer, an American journalist living in Germany, gave this verdict on the Nazis after the elections of 1928.

'Nazism appears to be a dying cause. It got support because of the country's problems such as hyperinflation and the French invasion of the Ruhr. Now that the country's outlook is bright it is dying away. One scarcely hears of Hitler except as the butt of jokes.'

Activities

3 Study Source B. Do you agree with Shirer's views about the Nazi Party in 1928? Explain your answer.

4 Make a copy of the following table and then complete it with some reasons that these three groups of people may have for supporting the Nazis.

Group	Possible reasons to support Nazis
Young people	
Farmers	
Merchants	

What effects did the depression have on Germany?

From October 1929, Germany was badly affected by an economic depression. This further weakened the Weimar Republic and provided Hitler and the Nazis with the ideal opportunity to increase their support.

Wall Street Crash
In October 1929 disaster struck the New York stock exchange on Wall Street. The value of the shares collapsed following a few days of wild speculation. Many US businesses were ruined and the Americans had no option but to end their loans to Germany and demand the repayment of existing loans.

German businessmen
Many German businesses were forced to close. They were heavily dependent on loans from the USA. To make matters worse, the government increased their taxes in order to pay for helping the rapidly increasing numbers of unemployed.

German workers
Many workers and farm labourers lost their jobs. By 1932, six million were out of work, including 40% of factory workers. At the same time the government cut unemployment benefit to save money. Many families suffered terrible poverty.

Weimar Republic
Most Germans blamed the Weimar Republic for allowing the German economy to become far too dependent on US loans. In addition, the government was criticised for its failure to deal with the worst effects of the depression, especially high unemployment.

German young people
Unemployment badly affected the young. By the end of 1932, half of Germans between sixteen and thirty could not find jobs, including 60% of university graduates.

Source A: A graph showing unemployment in Germany, 1928–1936.

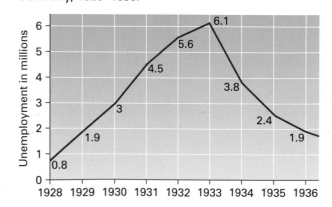

Activities

1 What was the **Wall Street Crash**?

2 Study Source A. When did unemployment reach its peak?

3 Make a list of at least three effects of the depression on Germany.

4 'The Weimar Republic was unable to manage economic problems in Germany in the years 1919–1932.' Discuss.

Source B: The writer Heinrich Hauser describes what he saw as he toured Germany in 1932.

'An almost unbroken chain of homeless men extends the whole length of the Hamburg–Berlin highway. It is the same scene for the entire two hundred miles, and all the highways in Germany over which I travelled this year. They walked separately or in small groups with their eyes on the ground. And they had the strange, stumbling gait of barefoot people, for their shoes were slung over their shoulders.'

Activities

5 What can you learn from Source B about the effects of the depression on Germany?

6 Who suffered the most during the depression? Explain your answer.

Why was the Weimar Republic weakened by the depression?

The Weimar Republic was weakened for several reasons.

- It lacked a strong leader to reduce the worst effects of the depression. Stresemann, who might have provided such strong leadership, died just a few weeks before the Wall Street Crash.
- The Weimar constitution had encouraged weak and short-lived coalitions, unable to provide solutions to major problems, and the depression highlighted these weaknesses.

Activities

7 'The Wall Street Crash was to blame for the economic and social problems of Germany in the years 1929–1932.'

From the evidence, how far do you agree or disagree with this opinion? Work in groups and consider the following:

- the impact of the Wall Street Crash
- German policies 1924–1929
- the actions of the Weimar governments 1929–1932.

Results Plus

Watch out!

Many students get confused between the Wall Street Crash of 1929 and hyperinflation in 1923. Make sure that you know the difference between the two. You will not receive any marks for writing about the wrong one in the exam!

- The two leading parties in the coalition government, the Centre Party and SDP, fell out with each other. Hermann Muller, the leader of the SDP, refused to agree to cuts in unemployment benefit, favoured by Heinrich Bruning, the leader of the Centre Party. Muller resigned, leaving Bruning as Chancellor, but without a majority in the Reichstag. Bruning asked President Hindenburg to use Article 48 of the Constitution which meant, in an emergency such as the depression, laws could be issued without having to go through the Reichstag.
- From 1930, Germany effectively ceased to be a democracy, as the Reichstag met less and less frequently, and it was seen as ineffective by many Germans. Moreover, the German government was now controlled by an 84-year-old President, an ex-army leader, who seemed well past his prime.
- To make matters worse, Bruning's government introduced unpopular economic policies to try to deal with the depression. They remembered the hyperinflation of 1923 and refused to increase government spending or print more money. Instead, the Chancellor raised taxes, which infuriated businessmen already suffering from the depression, reduced wages and made cuts in unemployment benefit.
- Many Germans now turned to support the more extreme parties, such as the communists and the Nazis, who seemed to offer possible solutions to the depression. The communists blamed the capitalist system and insisted that only a communist government could get Germany out of the depression. The Nazis, on the other hand, gave people scapegoats for Germany's economic problems – the Jews, the Weimar politicians and the communists.

KnowZone
The rise of the Nazi Party

Quick quiz

1 Are the following statements true or false? If they are false, what is the correct answer?

	True or false	Correct answer
The Spartacists were led by Karl Liebneckt and Rosa Luxemburg		
The Kapp Putsch failed because of the actions of the German army		
The 'stab in the back' theory suggested that Germany had lost the war		
The French occupied the Ruhr because Germany failed to make its reparations payments		
Everyone in Germany was badly affected by hyperinflation		
Hitler joined the German Workers Party in 1919		
The SA were known as the blackshirts		
The emblem of the Nazi Party was the swastika		
Passive resistance meant refusing to cooperate with the French		
German reparations payments were fixed at £3,300 million		

2 The following paragraph is not an accurate account of the period of recovery in the years 1924–1929.

(i) Find the errors.

(ii) Replace them with the correct answer.

> Gustav Stresemann was Chancellor of Germany throughout the years 1924 to 1929. He negotiated the Dawes Plan with Britain, by which German reparations payments were increased. In addition, Britain agreed to give loans to Germany. In 1925, Stresemann took Germany out of the League of Nations. In 1926, Germany signed the Locarno Treaties with neighbouring countries such as Belgium, Holland and France. Finally, in 1929, Stresemann negotiated the Young Plan with France. This further increased German reparations payments.

3 Match the following definitions to the words and phrases:

Words/phrases	Definitions
Reparations	German parliament
Reichstag	Money loses all value as prices soar
SA	German name for being forced to sign the peace treaty
Hyperinflation	Stormtroopers
The diktat	*My Struggle* – Hitler's autobiography
Polish Corridor	Parties given seats in parliament in proportion to number of votes
Mein Kampf	Area which split Germany into two
Proportional representation	Compensation for war damage

Checklist

How well do you know and understand?

- The early problems of the Weimar Republic.
- The reasons for early opposition to the Republic.
- How successful the Republic was in dealing with these problems and the opposition.
- The causes and effects of the hyperinflation of 1923.
- The importance of the Munich Putsch of 1923.
- How far the Weimar Republic recovered in the years 1924–1929.
- Which groups supported the Nazi Party in the years 1921–1928.
- Why there was greater support for the Nazis in the years 1929–1932.
- Which groups supported the Nazis in the years 1929–1932.

Plenary activities

Have you heard of a 'scatter graph'? This is often used to plot two sets of data and compare them. Here is an example of such a graph.

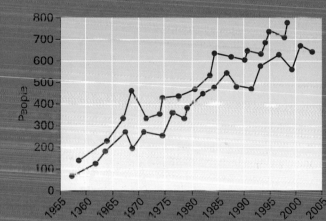

Make a copy of the following scatter graph.

1 In the following table are key developments in the Weimar Republic and Nazi Party.

- Find the key dates for each event.
- Plot each development above the appropriate year on your graph. If you think it was very beneficial then put it near the top ('Ups'). If you think it was disastrous then put it near the bottom ('Downs').
- Plot the developments in the Weimar Republic in blue on your graph.
- Plot developments in the Nazi Party in red.

2 Are there any patterns or links in your graph? Explain your answer.

Weimar Republic	Nazi Party
Dawes Plan	Hitler in prison
Hyperinflation	1928 election result
Spartacists	Hitler joins the German
Rentenmark	Workers Party
Treaty of Versailles	Munich Putsch
French occupation of the Ruhr	Nazi Party set up
	Beginning of SA
Kapp Putsch	Hitler reorganises the Nazi Party
Entry to League of Nations	Reorganisation of Nazi Party

KnowZone
Government of the Third Reich

Quick quiz

1 Place the following events in chronological order

a) The Reichstag Fire	
b) The Nazis win 105 seats in the Reichstag	
c) The Enabling Act	
d) Schleicher becomes Chancellor	
e) The Nazis win 196 seats in the Reichstag	
f) The Night of the Long Knives	
g) Hitler becomes Chancellor	
h) The Nazis win 230 seats in the Reichstag	
i) Trades Unions are banned	
j) Papen becomes Chancellor	
k) Germany becomes a one-party state	

2 The Nazis used a mixture of terror and persuasion to bring about support for the Nazi regime.

a) Make a copy of the following table.

Terror	Persuasion

b) Organise the following methods into categories, either terror or persuasion, and complete your copy of the table. Add more rows if you need to.

**radio Gestapo   concentration camps
Reich Church   Concordat with the Pope
SS   Nuremberg rallies   control of art
posters   cinema   cult of Fuhrer
one-party state**

3 Make a copy of the following account of opposition to the Nazis and use the words given below to complete the gaps:

It was very _____ to oppose the Nazi government. However, some groups and _____ were prepared to do this. One such group was the _____ _____ who were named after a flower. A second group, the _____ _____ _____ was set up during the Second World War. The leaders of both these groups were eventually captured and _____. A member of the army, Colonel _____ organised a plot to blow up Hitler. The bomb did go off but Hitler _____. Hitler was also opposed by Church leaders such as _____ _____. He was arrested for criticising the Nazi government and sent to a _____ camp.

**individuals   executed   Edelweiss Pirates
difficult   von Stauffenberg   pastor
concentration   Ludwig Niemöller   survived
White Rose Group**

Plenary activities

Work in groups on this activity.

The following individuals and groups helped or hindered Hitler in his rise to power and establishment of a dictatorship of the Nazi Party.

1 Make a copy of the following table.

Helped	Hindered

2 Categorise the following groups and individuals under the headings 'Helped' or 'Hindered' giving a brief explanation for each. (You may need to place some in both columns.)

**Hugenberg   communists   Hindenburg
SA   Papen   big business   Schleicher
Gestapo   Goebbels   Catholic Church
Röhm   Protestant Church**

Checklist

How well do you know and understand?

- The reasons why Hitler was invited to become Chancellor in January 1933.
- The methods Hitler used to remove opposition in the years 1933–1934.
- Hitler's role as Führer.
- The key features of the Nazi police state.
- Censorship and propaganda used by the Nazis.
- Nazi policies towards the Churches.
- Reasons for opposition to the Nazi government.
- The activities of opposition groups.
- The successes and failures of these opposition groups.

Student tip

Candidates often confuse the two command words 'Describe' and 'Explain'. If a question asks about an event:

- **Describe** means give precise details, generally in the correct sequence, of a key event.

- **Explain** is asking for developed causes or consequences of an event. For example, an explanation of the reasons for increased support for the Nazis in the years 1929–1932.

3.1 Nazi policies towards women and the young

Learning outcomes

By the end of this topic, you should be able to:

● understand Nazi policies towards women

● explain Nazi policies towards the young

● describe the successes and failures of these policies

Conscription: Compulsory military service

Eugenics: Study of improving the quality of the human race

Labour exchanges: Job centres

Lebensraum: Living space

Activities

1 Study the diagram below. Identify two things you can learn about women and their roles in Nazi Germany.

2 Write down three changes that women experienced under the Nazis.

Getting an overview

Appearance

The 1920s saw new fashions for women including short hair, make-up and shorter skirts. Women began to smoke and drink in public. The Nazis believed in the traditional natural appearance with long hair, no make-up and long skirts. Women were discouraged from smoking and drinking.

Employment

There had been progress in women's employment opportunities in the 1920s, especially in the more professional careers in teaching and medicine. The Nazis reduced the number of women, especially married women, in employment. However, due to rearmament, more women were employed in industry after 1937.

Marriage

Hitler wanted to increase the birth rate and encouraged German women to marry and have as many children as possible. Married couples were given loans based on the number of children they had.

Nazi aims

The Nazis believed in the traditional domestic role of women, which was to marry, have children and look after the home. Policies were designed to reinforce this. The Nazis were determined to turn the young into loyal Nazis and also train boys and girls for their different roles in later life.

Education

The Nazis used education and youth movements to control the lives of girls (and boys). Schooling and Nazi youth movements were used to prepare the young for their future roles in society – the girls for their domestic role and the boys for work and the army.

Women in Weimar Germany

There had been a number of changes in the position of women in Germany in the 1920s. In fact, Germany was ahead of Britain in political and employment rights for women.

- In 1919 women over the age of 20 were given the vote. This encouraged greater female interest in politics. Indeed by 1933 nearly one-tenth of Reichstag members were female.
- Many young women enjoyed much greater social freedom. They went out without a chaperone (someone to escort them) and smoked and drank in public places.
- There were major changes in their appearance. They wore short skirts, make-up and had their hair cut short.
- There was rapid progress in female employment opportunities. Many women now took up careers in the professions, especially the civil service and teaching. Indeed, in some careers women earned the same pay as men.

Source A: An advert for perfume from the 1920s that features the 'modern woman'.

Nazi aims

Source B: From Gertrud Scholtz-Klink, Head of the Nazi Women's Organisation.

'Woman is entrusted in the life of the nation with the great task, the care of man, soul, body and mind. It is the mission of woman to look after the home. Her role in marriage is as a comrade and helper to her husband – this is the right of woman in the New Germany.'

The Nazis wanted to reverse the developments of the 1920s so that women would return to their traditional role as homemakers and childbearers. This was for several reasons:

- Hitler genuinely believed in this traditional role, which he believed raised women to a very important place in society.
- Removing women from the job market would reduce the problem of unemployment.
- The Nazis were determined to increase the birth rate and strengthen the Third Reich.
- Women had a central role in producing the genetically pure Aryan race and the future Nazi warriors.
- The Nazi slogan 'Kinder, Kirche, Kuche' ('Children, Church, Cooking') summed up the role of women in Germany.

Source C: From an article published in Germany in 1933.

'There is no room for women who are interested in politics in Nazi Germany. All that this movement has ever said and thought on the subject goes against politics and women. Woman is relegated to her role as a mother and a wife. The German revolution is an event made by, and supremely concerned with, the male.'

Activity

1 What does Source B suggest about the role of women in Nazi Germany?

Women and employment

From 1933 women were encouraged to give up their jobs, get married and have large families. Women doctors, civil servants and teachers were forced to leave their jobs. **Labour exchanges** and employers were encouraged to give the first choice of jobs to men.

Girls were discouraged from going on to higher education, so that they would not have the qualifications for professional careers. Indeed, generous social security benefits were given to encourage women to stay at home.

Marriage and the family

In 1933 the Law for the Encouragement of Marriage was introduced. This provided loans to help young couples to marry, as long as the wife left her job. For each child, up to four children, couples were allowed to keep one-quarter of the loan. A number of other policies encouraged more births and laws against abortion were strictly enforced. Birth-control clinics were closed down and a massive propaganda campaign was launched to promote the importance of the mother and the family. The government also increased maternity benefits.

On Hitler's mother's birthday (12 August) medals were awarded to women with larger families:

● Gold for eight or more.
● Silver for six children.
● Bronze for five children.

Additionally, a new national organisation, called the German Women's Enterprise, organised classes and radio talks on household topics and the skills of motherhood.

Women's appearance

The ideal Nazi woman was fair-haired, blue-eyed and sturdily built. She was expected to have broad hips for childbearing and to wear traditional clothes, not fashionable ones. She would not wear make-up, nor did she smoke or drink. Slimming was frowned upon because being slim was considered bad for childbearing.

Activities

2 Explain how the Nazis changed the role of women in the years after 1933.

Source D: A poster produced in 1935 by the Organisation to Aid Mothers and Children. It says 'Germany grows through strong mothers and healthy children.'

Source E: A sketch by a Nazi artist showing the ideal Nazi woman.

How successful were the Nazi policies regarding women in achieving their aims?

There were successes. In the first few years the number of married women in employment fell. Moreover, the number of marriages increased and there was a rise in the birth rate. The German Women's Enterprise Organisation had 6 million members. It organised 'Mother's Schools' to train women in household skills, as well as courses, lectures and radio programmes on household topics.

For many women these were good times. Those who had been hardest hit by the depression were much better off by 1935. Those who had been able to find employment found that their wages were rising faster than prices.

However, there were limitations and even failures. The rise in the birth rate may have been due to the economic recovery of the period rather than Nazi policies. Most couples continued to have families of two children.

Moreover, the number of women in employment actually increased from 4.85 million in 1933 to 7.14 million six years later. From 1936, there was a labour shortage and the Nazis needed more workers in heavy industry because of rearmament. In 1937, the Nazis changed the marriage loans scheme to allow married women who had been given a loan to take up employment. Many employers preferred women workers because they were cheaper. Women's wages remained only two-thirds of a man's.

Source F: From a history of Germany 1918–1945, written in 1997.

'In their efforts the Nazis enjoyed some success. The numbers of working women only rose from 4.8 million in 1932 to 5.9 million in 1937, but because more men than women were taking jobs, this was really a fall from 37% to 31% of the total work force. But women were really too useful to the German economy to remove them completely from the work force. As the Nazis geared Germany up for war, women provided cheap and reliable labour. The Nazis relaxed the restrictions of women working from 1938. The Nazis were caught in the contradictions of their position.'

Source G: From a history of Germany, written in 2001.

'In some areas, such as women's organisations and youth groups, the Nazis widened the experiences for women. Social services improved. Opportunities to avoid the drudgeries of paid employment had advantages. Furthermore, many historians now stress the ineffectiveness of Nazi restrictions. That is not to deny that for many women (though proportionately a small number) as well as men the experience of the regime was horrific.'

Source H: Women's employment in millions.

Married women working outside the home	Total (millions)
1933	4.2
1939	6.2*

*35% of married women aged 16–65.

Job	1933	1939
Agriculture and forestry	4.6	4.9
Industry and crafts	2.7	3.3
Trade and transport	1.9	2.1
Non-domestic services	0.9	1.1
Domestic services	1.2	1.3

Activities

3 According to Sources F and G, did the position of women in Nazi Germany improve?

4 'Nazi policies towards women were a failure.' To what extent do you agree with this view? Working in pairs, evaluate the following:
   - the successes of the Nazi policies
   - the limitations and failures.
   Make a final assessment and give your reasons.

5 'Women in Nazi Germany were different, not inferior.' Discuss.

The Nazis and young people

Source A: Bernhard Rust, the Nazi Minister of Education.

'The whole purpose of education is to create Nazis.'

The Nazis were determined to turn the young into loyal Nazis. In addition they wanted to train boys and girls for their different roles in later life. It became compulsory for all teachers to be members of the Nazi Party, and they also had to swear an oath of loyalty to the Nazi Party. The Nazis tried to achieve this aim by controlling education during the weekdays and youth movements in the evenings and weekends.

Activities

1 What can you learn from Source A about the Nazis and education?
2 Write down one difference and two similarities in the education and youth movements of girls and boys.

Nazi control of education

The Nazis used education as a method of indoctrinating the young with Nazi ideas, that is, teaching them to accept their views. This was achieved by controlling all aspects of education.

The Nazis ensured that teachers accepted and taught Nazi ideals; those who did not were sacked. Many teachers attended teachers' camps, which concentrated on how to indoctrinate the young and on physical training. Nearly all teachers joined the Nazi Teachers' Association.

The curriculum was carefully organised to put across key Nazi ideals:

- Lessons began and ended with the teachers and pupils saluting and saying 'Heil Hitler'.
- History was rewritten to glorify Germany's past and the rise of the Nazi Party. History books attacked the Treaty of Versailles and blamed Jews and communists for Germany's past problems.
- Physical education occupied 15 per cent of school time to ensure that girls were fit to be mothers and boys were prepared for military service. Pupils had to pass a physical examination or else they could be expelled from school.
- **Eugenics** was a new subject that taught pupils about selective breeding, more especially the creation of a master race. Pupils were taught that they were not to marry inferior racial types, such as Jews.
- Race studies was another new subject. This put forward Nazi ideas of race, in particular the superiority of the Aryan race and the inferiority of the sub-humans, the Jews. Pupils were taught how to measure their skulls and to classify racial types.
- In geography pupils were taught about lands that were once part of Germany and the need for more *Lebensraum* (that is, land to inhabit) for Germans.

Nazi textbooks
From 1935, all textbooks had to be centrally approved by the Nazis. New textbooks were produced reflecting Nazi ideals.

Nazi schools
Everyone in Germany had to go to school until the age of 14. After that, schooling was optional. The Nazis moved away from co-education to separate schools and curriculums for the two sexes.

- Boys took science, maths and military drilling. Schooling for boys concentrated on physical fitness and military fitness and skills to prepare them for the armed forces.
- Girls took needlework, music, language and homecrafts. Female education was designed to prepare girls for marriage and motherhood with the emphasis on domestic duties as well as physical fitness.

Source B: Extract from a Nazi history textbook about a First World War battle.

'A Russian soldier tried to get in his way, but Otto's bayonet slid gratingly between his ribs, so that he collapsed groaning. There it lay before him, simple and distinguished, his dream's desire, the Iron Cross.'

Source C: A German father describes a mathematics question in his son's textbook.

'When Klauss got back from school at five o'clock he bullied me into helping him with his homework. Here is a maths problem picked out at random: "A plane on take off carries 12 bombs, each weighing 10 kilos. The aircraft makes for Warsaw, the centre of international Jewry. It bombs the town. On take-off with all the bombs on board and a fuel tank containing 1,500 kilos of fuel the aircraft weighed 8 tonnes. When it returned from the crusade, there were still 230 kilos of fuel left. What is the weight of the aircraft when empty?"'

Source D: An illustration from a textbook shows a Jewish 'sex-fiend' passing out sweets to children.

„Hier, Kleiner, haft du etwas ganz Süßes! Aber dafür müßt ihr beide mit mir gehen…"

![Results Plus — Build better answers]

Give two examples of things that you can learn from Source D about education in Nazi Germany. (4 marks)

Basic, Level 1 (1–2 marks)
Answer makes an inference but does not use the source to support it, for example: the Nazis were against the Jews or they used propaganda.

Good, Level 2 (3–4 marks)
Answer uses the source to support the inference. For example, the source shows that propaganda was used in education. There was propaganda against the Jews in school textbooks, where the Jew is shown as an ugly 'sex-fiend'. The Jewish man is shown as a danger to children to encourage hatred of Jews.

3.2 Economic changes in Nazi Germany

Learning outcomes

By the end of this topic you should be able to:

- understand Nazi attempts to reduce unemployment
- explain Nazi economic policies
- describe the standard of living enjoyed by the German people under the Nazis

Autarky: Self-sufficiency

Autobahns: German motorways

Invisible unemployed: Unemployed not counted in official figures

Real wages: Wages adjusted to allow for inflation

Rearmament: Building up armed forces and weapons

Getting an overview

The Nazis were determined to reduce unemployment and build up the German armaments industry in readiness for a future war.

1933 Job creation schemes, especially the building of autobahns.

1934 Many women were forced to give up their jobs.

1935 National Labour Service was compulsory for all men between the age of 18 and 25. They spent six months working on public works schemes such as road building. Conscription was introduced for the German armed forces.

1936 Many Jews had been forced from their jobs.

1937 Rearmament led to the expansion of heavy industries such as iron and steel, coal, engineering, shipbuilding and the manufacture of tanks and military aircraft and more jobs.

1938 Over one third of German spending was on rearmament which created more and more jobs.

1939 The German army had grown from 100,000 in 1933 to 1,400,000.

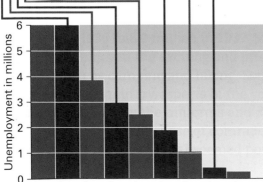

Better off	Worse off
In some ways Germans were better off under Hitler:	In other ways Germans were worse off under Hitler:
• Most German men were in work • The 'Strength through Joy' organisation provided better leisure activities and holidays for workers • The 'Beauty of Labour' department improved working conditions, e.g. canteens and sports facilities • Average weekly wages rose from 86 marks in 1932 to 109 marks in 1939 • The Volkswagen Scheme of 1938 gave workers the chance to buy cheap cars	• Trades Unions were abolished and workers had few rights • Few workers could afford the more expensive activities and holidays provided by Strength through Joy • Most German men did not enjoy National Labour Service, which was poorly paid • The cost of living went up in the 1930s – this cancelled out the rise in wages • Average hours of work went up from 43 hours per week in 1933 to 47 in 1939 • The Volkswagen scheme turned out to be a swindle

Activities

1 Identify three ways in which the Nazis reduced unemployment.

2 Give two examples of people being better off and two examples of people being worse off.

Nazi economic policies

German economic policy was dominated by two men and their plans:

- Dr Hjalmar Schacht: the New Plan (1933–1937); and
- Hermann Göring: the Four Year Plan (1936–1940).

Schacht and the New Plan

Dr Hjalmar Schacht was made President of the Reichsbank in 1933 and, the following year, Minister of the Economy. His aims were to:

- Reduce unemployment.
- Make Germany self-sufficient so it could survive future wars even if it was blockaded: this policy was known as **autarky**.

To achieve these he introduced the 'New Plan'. This plan was successful because it coincided with a revival in the world economy. Schacht succeeded in limiting German imports. He also made trade agreements with individual countries, by which they supplied Germany with essential raw materials in return for German goods. By 1935, Germany had a small trade surplus and production had increased by 50 per cent since 1933.

Schacht, however, was removed from his job in 1937 because he spoke against Hitler's plans to rearm quickly, arguing that the economy was not strong enough.

Göring and the Four Year Plan

From 1936, Germany's economic policy was increasingly controlled by Hermann Göring, a leading Nazi, who had little knowledge of the economy. His Four Year Plan dealt with preparing Germany for war within four years. The whole economy was geared towards **rearmament** and to making Germany self-sufficient in essential war materials, such as rubber, oil and steel.

The government poured millions of marks into the Four Year Plan. Business was persuaded to produce synthetic raw materials such as rubber, fuel and textiles. Textiles were made from pulped wood, rubber from coal, coffee from

Source A: A poster encouraging German workers to help in the struggle for autarky. It says 'Help Hitler build. Buy German goods'.

acorns and petrol from coal. However, these were not very successful and, in 1939, Germany was still dependent on foreign imports for its raw materials and oil.

New industrial plants, such as the Hermann Göring Works, which was a huge mining and metal works, were set up. Many of these used forced labour from the concentration camps. Arms production was given priority over consumer goods and agriculture. However, this led to food shortages and, in 1939, butter was still being rationed in Germany.

In fact the only way Germany could become fully self-sufficient was through foreign invasion and conquest. Some historians believe that the Four Year Plan was in crisis by 1939 and this forced Hitler to invade Poland.

Activities

1 What is the message of Source A?
2 Which plan, the New Plan or the Four Year Plan, was more successful in achieving its aims? Explain your answer.

How did the Nazis reduce unemployment?

When he became Chancellor in 1933, Hitler was determined to reduce unemployment and carry out the promises he had made in the years 1929–1932. In 1933, unemployment stood at 6 million and had fallen to less than half a million six years later. His policies seemed to have been more successful than those carried out by Britain, where unemployment fell from 3 million in 1939 to just under half that number in 1939. Germany's success was the result of several policies.

Job creation schemes

These were not new. The Weimar Republic had introduced a number of public works programmes in the years 1929–1933. Hitler, also, sought to create jobs through government spending on construction. In 1933, 18.4 billion marks was spent on these schemes, rising to 37.1 billion by 1938.

Germany built a network of motorways, known as **autobahns**, covering 7,000 km. This not only provided jobs, but also improved the efficiency of German industry by increasing the speed at which goods could cross the country, as well as enabling the swift transport of German troops. In addition, huge public buildings were constructed, for example, the stadium in Berlin for the 1936 Olympics.

The Nazis also subsidised private firms, especially in the construction industry, to stimulate the economy and provide more jobs. They invested money in the car industry, producing the Volkswagen or 'People's Car'. The German car industry as a whole expanded, which created jobs and reduced foreign car imports.

Source A: A poster promoting the Deutsche Arbeitsfront (DAF) or German Labour Front (see page 85). It says 'We Remain Comrades'.

National Labour Service

The National Labour Service was also not new. It had been started by the Weimar Republic and was continued by the Nazis. It was known as the *Reichsarbeitsdienst* or RAD and, in July 1935, it was made compulsory for all men aged between 18 and 25, who had to serve six months. This provided men to build the autobahns, as well as labour for other projects: for example, draining marshes to be used for farmland, tree planting, and building coastal walls to protect coastal areas from flooding.

The RAD removed thousands from the national unemployment figures. However, it was not popular. The workers were paid very low wages, and had to put up with uncomfortable tented camps, long hours of work and boring jobs.

Source B: A German remembers Labour Service.

'We work outdoors in all kinds of weather, shoveling dirt for very low pay. I'm trained as a printer. In the summer of 1933 I lost my job. I collected the dole until the spring of 1934. That was a lot better than what I am doing now. At least I was at home, with my family and could pick up odd jobs and work in the garden. Now I only get 10 day's holiday a year.'

Invisible unemployment

The official government figures did not include a number of groups who lost their jobs or those in labour service without proper jobs. These people became the **invisible unemployed**.

Activities

1 Identify two things you can learn from Source A on the opposite page about the aims of the Labour Service.

2 Working in pairs, produce a mind map showing the main reasons why unemployment fell in Germany in the years 1933–1939.

 • Prioritise the reasons within your mind map, beginning with the most important directly above the central box (at 12 o'clock) and then work your way round clockwise to finish with the least important.

 • Explain your most important and least important reasons.

 • Draw lines showing links between these reasons. Explain the links.

3 'Nazi policies hid, rather than reduced, the numbers out of work.' Discuss.

Jews
From 1933, more and more Jews were forced out of their jobs, especially in the professions, such as lawyers and doctors.

Women
Many women were dismissed from their jobs, especially in professional jobs. Others were tempted by state marriage loans to give up their jobs and marry.

Unmarried men
Unmarried men under the age of 25 were forced to serve six months in National Labour Service.

Opponents
In the early years of the Nazi government many opponents of Nazism, especially communists, were arrested and sent to concentration camps.

Rearmament

Rearmament became especially important in the years after 1936. The Four Year Plan changed the whole emphasis of the economy to preparing for a future war. The drive for rearmament created more jobs as more money was spent on manufacturing weapons. Billions were spent producing tanks, ships and aircraft. Heavy industry especially benefited. In the years 1933–1939, production of coal and chemicals doubled, oil and iron and steel trebled, and iron ore extraction increased five-fold.

In addition, the expansion of the armed forces provided more jobs. When Hitler came to power the army was limited to just 100,000 men. By 1938, the figure had risen to 900,000.

Beauty of Labour

Known as the SdA, Beauty of Labour was another branch of the German Labour Front. Its main task was to improve working conditions, such as, for example, reducing the noise levels of machines. It also organised the building of canteens, swimming pools and sports facilities as well as better heating. Nevertheless, workers were expected to make these improvements in their spare time. This made the scheme less popular with many workers.

The Volkswagen

The scheme to build the Volkswagen was another function of the KdF. Hitler was keen to expand car ownership and encouraged the development of a new car, the Volkswagen, which means 'people's car'. It was to be cheap enough for workers to afford. A scheme was introduced in which workers paid 5 marks a week towards the cost of buying the car. However, by the time war broke out, not a single car had been bought and none of the money was refunded.

In 1939 production of the Volkswagen was switched to the needs of the military.

Source F: Hitler introducing the Volkswagen, 1938.

How well off were other groups under the Nazis?

Farming communities

The Nazis had gained strong support from farmers in the years after 1927. They flattered them with propaganda slogans, such as 'Blood and Soil'. Some farm debts were written off, and all farmers benefited from a rise in food prices. Farmers however suffered from a shortage of labour because workers left for better jobs in the towns.

Small business

The Nazis had also received much support from those in the small business sector, such as shopkeepers and craftsmen. The Nazis had promised to curb the influence of the large department stores and passed laws that banned the growth of the existing stores.

Big business

Big business really benefited from Nazi rule. There was no longer the worry about troublesome Trades Unions and the possibility of strikes. Rearmament resulted in growth and larger profits. Companies such as IG Farben gained huge government contracts to make explosives and even artificial oil from coal. The average salary of managers increased by nearly 70 per cent in the years 1934 to 1938. However, some industrialists did resent Nazi control of wages, profits, imports and raw materials.

Source A: M. Collier and P. Pedley, *Germany 1918–45*, published in 2001.

'Most workers enjoyed real wage rises after 1933 and skilled workers prospered with a return to full employment by 1936. At the same time the working week increased from an average of 40 hours in 1933 to 60 hours in 1944. Industrial accidents and industrial related illnesses rose by 150 per cent between 1933 and 1939. In addition, there was some working class unrest. There were strikes at Russelheim and Berlin in 1936 and a Party report from Nuremberg found open insubordination, sabotage, go-slows and absenteeism.'

Source B: W. Simpson, *Hitler and Germany*, published in 1991.

'The success or failure of Hitler's economic policies has been the subject of much debate. Unemployment was certainly cured, though whether this was due to a natural upturn in the world economy, work-creation schemes or rearmament is open to question. Heavy industry, iron and steel and chemicals showed a massive growth. The German Labour Front, through its promotion of organizations like "Strength through Joy" and "The Beauty of Labour", may have improved working conditions. But real wages barely rose between 1933 and 1939. Rearmament did not provide the resources for a large-scale war.'

ResultsPlus

Top tip!

You will gain marks by supporting your exam answers with examples. For this topic, this means being able to give some examples of job creation schemes and other ways in which unemployment was reduced.

Activities

1   Make a copy of and complete the following table, using Sources A and B.

Successes of Nazi policies	Shortcomings of Nazi policies

2   How successful were Nazi economic policies? You will need to consider the achievements and shortcomings of:
   • the policies of Schacht and Göring
   • measures to reduce unemployment
   • the standard of living.

3   'The Nazis sacrificed living standards in order to prepare for war.' Discuss.

Summary

● The Nazis were determined to make Germany self-sufficient. Schacht began a policy of autarky. This was continued with Göring's Four Year Plan.

● Unemployment was removed in the years 1933–1939 through rearmament, the Labour Service and 'invisible unemployment'.

● In some respects workers were better off under the Nazis because of Beauty of Labour and Strength through Joy.

● In other respects they were worse off because of the banning of trades unions and the Volkswagen swindle.

1933
6 million out of work
Trades unions banned
Introduction of the Labour Front

1934
Schacht made Minister of the Economy

1935
Reich National Service Law

1936
Beginning of Göring's Four Year Plan

1938
Beginning of the Volkswagen scheme

1939
300,000 out of work

3.3 Nazi treatment of minorities

Learning outcomes

By the end of this topic you should be able to:

● understand Nazi racial policies

● explain Nazi policies towards minorities including the Jews

● describe the Final Solution

Getting an overview

The Nazis were determined to create a master race of **Aryans** – tall, fair-haired and blue-eyed. This would be achieved through selective breeding. At the same time, Hitler was determined to eliminate what he saw as inferior races, such as the Jews.

Anti-Semitism: Opposition to and attack on Jews

Aryan: Nazi term for someone of supposedly pure Germanic stock

Final Solution: The Nazi policy to exterminate all Jews in Europe

Ghetto: An area of a city or town used for one racial group

Untermenschen: German word for sub-humans, including Jews and Slavs

Activities

1 Identify two things you can learn from Source A about Nazi views of the Jews.

2 Find three examples of how the treatment of Jews got worse from 1933–1939.

Source A: An illustration from a children's textbook. It shows Jewish people leaving Germany. The sign reads 'One way street'.

Nazi racial views

Central to Nazi policy was the creation of a pure German state. The Nazis divided the different races into two groups: the *Herrenvolk*, or master race, and the *Untermenschen*, 'sub-humans'.

The 'master race'

The Nazis believed that the Germans were of pure Aryan descent, from the *Herrenvolk* or 'master race'. They were depicted as being very Scandinavian looking – tall, blue-eyed, blond-haired and athletic.

Source A: Profile of the ideal Aryan male, who is hard-working.

Source B: From a speech by Heinrich Himmler, Head of the SS, in 1935.

'The first principle for us was and is the recognition of the values of blood and selection. We sorted out the people whom we thought unsuitable for the formation of the SS simply on the basis of outward appearances.'

Hitler wanted to create a master race through selective breeding. The SS were central to the drive for selective breeding and only recruited men who were of Aryan blood. In other words, they were tall, fair-haired and blue-eyed. They could only marry women of pure Aryan blood. Indeed, there were race farms all over Germany to breed Aryan children. Here, members of the SS and women of pure Aryan stock bred the pure Aryan master race of the future.

Source C: From the Nazi weekly magazine *Racial Research*.

'We demand of a member of this noble race that he marry only a blue-eyed, oval-faced, red-cheeked and thin-nosed blonde woman. We demand that he take a wife, a virgin only. We demand that the blue-eyed Aryan hero marry an Aryan girl who like himself is of pure and unblemished past.'

The *Untermenschen*

Other races, especially Jews and Slavs, people from Eastern Europe, were seen as inferior or sub-humans. Nazi policy was that they should be removed in case they prevent the creation of the pure Aryan master race.

Hitler had used the Jews as the scapegoat for Germany's problems after 1918: the 'stab in the back' theory, the humiliating Treaty of Versailles, and the hyperinflation of 1923. There were only half a million Jews in Germany in 1933, fewer than one person in every hundred. However, they did make up 16 per cent of all lawyers and 10 per cent of all doctors. Many Germans were jealous of their success and suspicious of their very different religion. This made Jews easy targets for Hitler's policy of **anti-Semitism**.

Activities

1 What can you learn from Source C about Nazi views on race?
2 For what reasons did the Nazis persecute the Jews?

Treatment of minorities

The Nazis wanted Germans who could contribute to society through work, military service or motherhood. Everyone else was seen as a 'burden on the community'. This included the severely disabled, mentally ill, and unhealthy. They were not only worthless to society, but expensive to look after. Others, such as vagrants and gypsies, were seen as undesirables and a bad influence.

90

Activities

1. To what extent were Nazi policies towards minority groups such as gypsies, vagrants and the mentally ill determined by their views on race?

2. Explain why gypsies, vagrants and the work-shy were persecuted by the Nazis.

Treatment of minorities

Gypsies

Gypsies were seen as a real threat because they were non-Aryan and thought to be work-shy. Although there were only 30,000 in Germany, the Nazis were determined to prevent them from mixing with Aryans. In 1935, marriages between gypsies and Aryans were banned. In 1938, a decree for the 'Struggle against the Gypsy Plague' was issued. This forced gypsies to register so they could be controlled.

Source A: Dr Ritter, head of the Nazi Institute of Criminal Biology.

'The gypsy question can be considered solved only when the majority of the asocial and unproductive gypsies are placed in large work camps and the further reproduction of this half-caste population is terminated.'

Black people

Black people were seen as *Untermenschen* too. The Nuremberg Laws of 1935 banned marriage between German Aryans and black people. The Nazis treated black people in much the same way as gypsies. Indeed they sterilized any children who were born to German women by black soldiers who had been stationed in the Rhineland after the First World War.

Vagrants

Vagrants included beggars, men moving from town to town trying to find work and young people who had left home. The Nazis forced these groups to work. In 1938 the SS rounded up 100,000 vagrants and placed them in concentration camps.

Source B: SS Officer Greifelt in January 1939.

'In view of the tight situation on the labour market, national labour discipline dictated that all persons who would not conform to the working life of the nation, and who were vegetating as work-shy and asocial, making the streets of our cities and countryside unsafe, had to be compulsorily registered and set to work. More than 10,000 of these asocial forces are currently undertaking a labour training cure in the concentration camps.'

Mentally ill

The Nazis were convinced that mental illness was hereditary and could not be cured. Therefore, they sterilised those believed to be mentally ill. By 1945, nearly 300,000 mentally ill people had been sterilised. However, the Nazis' actions became even more extreme after the outbreak of the Second World War. They set up the 'Public Ambulance Service Ltd' to kill the mentally ill. By 1945, it had murdered 70,000.

Treatment of Jews, 1933–1939

The Nazis were determined to force the Jews to leave Germany through a policy of persecution.

Anti-Jewish propaganda

The cinema, posters, newspapers and even school textbooks were all used to portray the Jews as evil moneylenders who were not to be trusted.

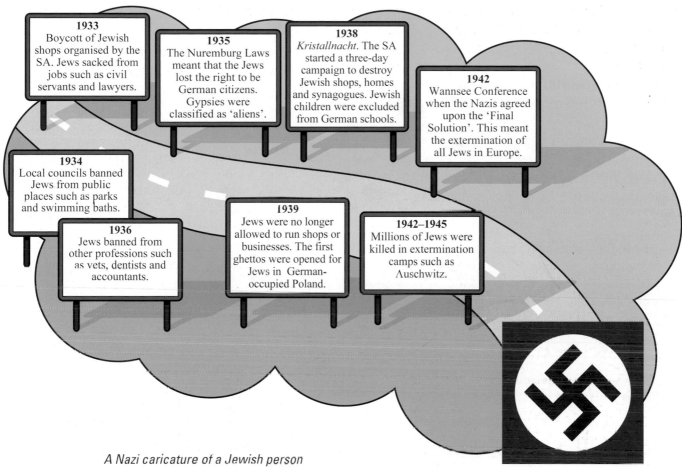

1933 Boycott of Jewish shops organised by the SA. Jews sacked from jobs such as civil servants and lawyers.

1934 Local councils banned Jews from public places such as parks and swimming baths.

1935 The Nuremburg Laws meant that the Jews lost the right to be German citizens. Gypsies were classified as 'aliens'.

1936 Jews banned from other professions such as vets, dentists and accountants.

1938 *Kristallnacht*. The SA started a three-day campaign to destroy Jewish shops, homes and synagogues. Jewish children were excluded from German schools.

1939 Jews were no longer allowed to run shops or businesses. The first ghettos were opened for Jews in German-occupied Poland.

1942 Wannsee Conference when the Nazis agreed upon the 'Final Solution'. This meant the extermination of all Jews in Europe.

1942–1945 Millions of Jews were killed in extermination camps such as Auschwitz.

A Nazi caricature of a Jewish person

Jews portrayed as evil-looking with particularly large noses

Reference to the wealth of Jews. Many Germans were resentful of Jews who were well off

To show the different customs of dress so Germans would regard them as outsiders or aliens

The Nazis encouraged Germans to believe that the Jews were close allies of international communism. This encouraged big business to support the Nazis and turn against Jewish businesses

To create an image of cruelty and savagery

Source A: From a history textbook used in a German school in 1942.

The Jewish race is much inferior to the Negro race.

All Jews have crooked legs, fat bellies, curly hair and look untrustworthy.

The Jews were responsible for the First World War.

They are to blame for the armistice of 1918 and the Versailles Treaty.

They caused the inflation of 1923.

They brought about the downfall of the Roman Empire.

Karl Marx is a great criminal.

All Jews are communists.

They are rulers of Russia.

Attacks on property

Within a few months of becoming Chancellor in March 1933 Hitler ordered the SA to turn customers away from Jewish shops. They also smashed windows in some Jewish shops and painted 'Jude' (Jew) on doors and windows. This boycott was extended to Jewish lawyers and doctors all over Germany.

Source B: Official statement from the Nazi Party, 30 March 1933.

'Boycott Committees against the Jews throughout the whole Reich. On 1 April, at the stroke of ten, the boycott of all Jewish businesses, doctors, lawyers begins – ten thousand mass gatherings. The Jews have declared war on 65 millions, now they are to be hit where it hurts them most.'

Source C: SA and SS men carrying out the boycott of Jewish shops in 1933.

During the summer of 1933, placards appeared outside shops, cafes, swimming pools, parks and many other public places throughout Germany saying either 'Jews not wanted' or 'Jews forbidden'.

In 1937, the Aryanisation of Jewish businesses was stepped up. More and more Jewish businesses were confiscated. In April 1938, Jews had to register their property, thus making it easier to confiscate. Finally, in 1939, Jews were no longer allowed to run shops or businesses.

Loss of jobs

In 1933, Hitler ordered the sacking from government jobs of anyone not of Aryan descent. Thousands of Jewish civil servants were immediately sacked. Nazi school authorities sacked Jewish teachers. Jewish actors and musicians were forbidden to perform in public. In May 1935, Jews were forbidden to join the army.

In 1936, the professional activities of Jews were banned or restricted. This included vets, dentists, accountants, surveyors, teachers and nurses. Two years later, Jewish doctors, dentists and lawyers were forbidden to treat or work for Aryans and effectively they could only deal with Jewish people.

Loss of social position

The social position of Jews was also systematically undermined by the Nazis. In 1934, local councils banned Jews from public places such as parks, playing fields and swimming pools. In 1938, Jewish children were excluded from German schools and universities. Jews with non-Jewish first names had to add and use the name 'Israel' for males and 'Sarah' for females. They also had to have the red letter 'J' stamped on their passports.

In the same year, Jews were banned from all theatres, shows, concert and lecture halls, museums, amusement places and sports fields. In the following year, they were no longer allowed to own radios or to buy cakes and chocolate.

The Nuremberg Laws

The Nuremberg Laws were passed in 1935 and denied Jews the basic right of German citizenship. The Reich Citizenship Law made Jews 'subjects' rather than citizens. In other words, the Jews lost the right to vote and to hold government office. The Law for the Protection of German Blood and Honour banned marriages between Jews and Aryans and forbade any sexual relations outside marriage.

Source D: A caricature of a Jew with the words 'Jews not welcome'. This was placed at the entrance to a beer hall.

Kristallnacht

The most violent actions taken against the Jews in the years 1933–1939 occurred on 9–10 November 1938. This followed the murder of Ernst von Rath, a secretary in the German embassy in Paris, by Herschel Grynspan, a Polish Jew. At a reunion of those involved in the Munich Putsch, Goebbels seized on this event as an excuse to suggest a campaign of terror against the Jews. Hitler agreed.

Source E: Instructions from the Reich Central Bureau for Security, November 1938.

'Only such measures may be employed as will not endanger German lives or property – for example, synagogues may only be burnt when there is no risk that fire will spread to neighbouring structures. Jewish stores and dwellings may be destroyed but not plundered. The police must not interfere with the demonstrations that will occur. Only as many Jews – particularly wealthy ones – should be arrested as can be accommodated in available jails.'

This led to *Kristallnacht* (Night of Broken Glass), 9–10 November 1938, so called because of the thousands of Jewish shop windows that were smashed, with over 815 shops destroyed, 191 synagogues set on fire and 76 synagogues demolished. Additionally, 91 Jews were killed and a further 20,000 arrested.

Many Germans watched the events of *Kristallnacht* with alarm and concern. However, the Nazi-controlled press presented it as a spontaneous reaction of ordinary Germans against Jews. Most Germans did not believe this, but hardly anyone protested for fear of arrest and death.

To make matters worse, Göring required Jews to meet the cost of damage to their property themselves. On 12 November 1938, the Jewish community was ordered to pay a fine of 1 billion Reichsmarks. On the same day, a decree was issued barring Jews from owning or managing businesses.

Activities

3 Working in pairs, make a copy of the following table.

	Rating 1–10	Explanation
Property		
Jobs		
Social position		
Nuremberg Laws		

a) Give each area of Jewish persecution a score of 1 to 10 to indicate how serious it was in affecting the position of Jews (1 = not serious at all, 10 = very serious).

b) Give a brief explanation of each choice.

4 Explain the importance of the Nuremberg Laws for the position of the Jews in Germany.

5 In what ways did the position of German Jews change in the years 1933–1938?

6 Was *Kristallnacht* due to popular German anti-Semitism? Explain your answer.

The Final Solution

Shortly before the outbreak of the Second World War, the persecution of the Jews in Germany had intensified. In January 1939, the Reich Central Office for Jewish Emigration was set up with Reinhard Heydrich as its director. The aim was forced emigration of German Jews. However, at this stage, the Nazis did not seem to have considered the mass slaughter of Jews.

The outbreak of war changed Nazi attitudes to the Jewish question in three ways.

1. It allowed a more extreme treatment of the Jews without concern for world opinion.
2. Early German successes increased the number of Jews under Nazi control and removed the very areas they had hoped to use for forced emigration.
3. Finally, it meant that the Nazis had to come up with more extreme solutions, especially because of the 3 million Jews in German-occupied west Poland.

Ghettos

Ghettos were the first solution. The Nazis gathered all the Jews into ghettos or 'Jewish reservations' in towns. Walls were built to keep them in. The largest ghetto was in Warsaw. The Germans allowed only starvation rations in to the ghettos, and thousands died from hunger, the intense cold or the disease typhus. About 55,000 died in the Warsaw ghetto.

Source A: A survivor remembers her first days in the Vilna ghetto in Poland.

'As we entered, we were directed to a house that would have been occupied by a family of four to six people under normal conditions. Now 25 to 30 of us were crammed in. Everybody was searching for a place to sleep. I was lucky. My mother found an empty space under a table and that became my bed. Going to the synagogue, praying and studying about our religion were absolutely forbidden. The Germans wanted to break the Jewish spirit and morale. Many people lost their will to live, but I was too stubborn to give in.'

Einstatzgruppen

In June 1941, the Germans invaded Russia. The Nazis organised special murder squads known as the *Einstatzgruppen*, who moved into Russia behind the advancing German armies with the express purpose of rounding up and killing Jews. They raided towns and villages and picked out any Jews, who were then marched to the outskirts of villages, forced to dig their own graves, and then shot. By 1943, it is estimated that the *Einstatzgruppen* had murdered over 2 million Russians, mainly Jews.

Source B: Women and girls from Dvinsk about to be shot by the *Einstatzgruppen*.

Activities

1. Give an example of one change in Nazi policy towards Jews after the outbreak of the Second World War.
2. Study Source A. Give two examples of the harsh treatment of Jews in ghettos.

Wannsee Conference

In the summer of 1941, a decision was taken by senior Nazi leaders to seek a permanent and final solution to the Jewish question. It was to exterminate them in death camps. Although Göring signed the order, it seems to have been mainly the idea of Himmler as a means of dealing with the problem of the increasing number of Jews in German-occupied areas.

Source C: Auschwitz Commandant Rudolf Höss writing in 1959.

'In the summer of 1941, I cannot remember the exact date, Himmler received me and said in effect: "The Fuhrer has ordered that the Jewish question be solved once and for all. The Jews are the sworn enemies of the German people and must be eradicated. Every Jew that we can lay our hands on is to be destroyed now during the war, without exception. If we cannot obliterate the biological basis of Jewry, the Jews will one day destroy the German people."'

In January 1942, leading Nazis met at Wannsee in Berlin to work out the details of the 'Final Solution'. Death camps were built in Poland, far away from Germany, where Jews were to be worked to death. Work on building gas chambers and crematoria at camps was accelerated. The first camp began operating on 17 March 1942 at Belzec on the eastern Polish border. By the summer of 1943, Jews from all over Europe were being transported to these camps.

The death camps

On arrival at the death camps, the Jews were divided into two groups. Those who were fit were put to work. The others were sent to the gas chambers. However, those who were put to work were not much better off: they were worked to death in the labour camps.

Older women, mothers with small children, pregnant women and children under 10 were usually taken away immediately to be executed. Young boys would lie about their age and invent a skill or craft in order to be given work and stay alive.

Source D: Camps in Germany and Poland.

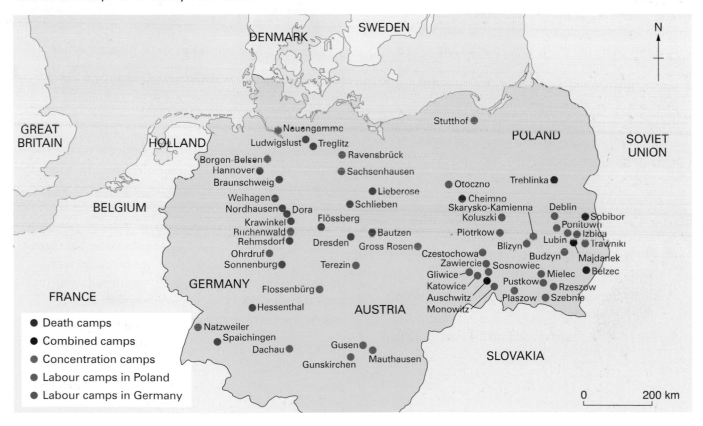

Source E: Errikos Sevillias describes his arrival at Auschwitz.

'As we huddled together, the SS quickly separated the men from the women. They took the old and the sick and put them in a special line… The doctor who examined me held my arm down on a table and tattooed it with the number 182699. My entire body was shaved, then I was given a shower and afterwards issued with clothes which had huge red painted marks on them. This was so I could be easily spotted if I tried to escape.'

Many died in the gas chambers from carbon monoxide and Zyclon B gasses. The Nazi aim was to carry out the **Final Solution** as efficiently as possible. For example at Treblinka, 140,000 were killed each month in 1942. Most gas chambers were fitted out as showers so that the prisoners would not realise what was happening to them. Bodies were burnt in ovens or left in mass pits.

Source F: Höss, the Commandant of Auschwitz, giving evidence at a trial after the war.

'I had to watch coldly while mothers with laughing children went into the gas chamber. I had to see everything. I had to watch hour by hour, by night by day, the burning and the removal of the bodies, the extraction of the teeth, the cutting of the hair, the whole grisly business. In the face of such grim considerations I was forced to bury all human feelings as deeply as possible.'

Activities

3 Study Sources E and G. What do they suggest about life in an extermination camp?

4 Study Source F. What justification does Höss give for his actions?

5 Why did the Nazis decide on the Final Solution?

Source G: Roll call at Auschwitz-Birkenau drawn by a prisoner, Ella Liebermann.

Prisoners who were not gassed were given various jobs to do, the worst being the removal of the dead bodies from the gas chambers. There was a strict daily routine, with roll calls for several hours per day before forced labour in mines or factories. The conditions were terrible. Food, which consisted of bread and thin soup, was very scarce. Diseases spread quickly. In addition, some inmates were used for medical experiments generally without anaesthetics. (Doctors were experimenting to create the perfect Aryan type.)

By the time the camps were liberated by the Allies in 1945, 6 million Jews and 500,000 European gypsies, as well as countless other prisoners, had been worked to death, gassed or shot.

Source H: A German policeman testifying in 1961.

'I believed the propaganda that all Jews were criminals and sub-humans and that they were the cause of Germany's decline after the First World War. The thought that one should disobey or evade the order to participate in the extermination of the Jews did not therefore enter my mind at all.'

Source I: From a school history textbook, written in 1997.

'There was little German opposition to these aspects of the Nazis' work because Hitler had been so effective in removing all opposition within Germany and placing Nazis in positions of power. Germans were subjected to a constant barrage of anti-Semitic propaganda. Some believed it. Of some things, Germans were simply not told. For many ordinary Germans who felt powerless to resist the persecution of the Jews, they consoled themselves with the thought that this was the price they had to pay for all the "benefits" of Hitler's rule.'

Activities

6 Why do you think there is no direct evidence of when the decision to carry out the Final Solution was taken?

7 In what ways did the Nazi treatment of the Jews change in the years 1939–1945? You may use the following in your answer and any other information of your own:

- Ghettos
- *Einstatzgruppen*
- Final Solution.

8 'The German people were responsible for the Final Solution.' Discuss.

Results Plus
Watch out!

It is important not just to focus on Nazi treatment of the Jews, unless the question specifically asks you to do so. To explain Nazi policies and ideology you need to mention all the types of people that were seen as inferior to the Nazi ideal.

Summary

- The Nazi theory of race was to create an Aryan master race and to remove the *Untermenschen* or sub-humans, such as the Jews.
- The Nazis were determined to remove anybody who was not of use to the regime. This included gypsies and the mentally ill.
- Hitler gradually introduced a series of measures aimed at forcing Jews to leave Germany. These included the Nuremberg Laws of 1935 and *Kristallnacht*.
- The outbreak of the Second World War meant that the Nazis had to change their policies towards the Jews from ghettos, to murder squads, to the Final Solution, carried out in specially built extermination camps.

1933
Boycott of Jewish shops

1934
Jews banned from public places

1935
Gypsies classified as aliens. Nuremberg Laws

1937
Jewish businesses taken over by the Nazis

1938
Kristallnacht

1939
Setting up of ghettos for Jews

1941
Setting up of *Einstatzgruppen*

1942
Wannsee Conference and Final Solution

1942–1945
Use of extermination camps to gas Jews

1945
Liberation of camps by Allies

Quick quiz

1 How good is your knowledge of German terms? What do the following terms mean?

Deutsches Jungvolk

Jung Madel

Autobahns

Autarky

Schönheit der Arbeit

Kraft durch Freude

2 In each row a)–g) in the following table, identify which term is the odd one out. Explain your choice.

			Odd one out	Reason
a) Jews	Gypsies	Germans		
b) Jews lose jobs	Labour Service	Invisible unemployment		
c) Race studies	Maths	Eugenics		
d) *Untermenschen*	Blond	Aryan race		
e) League of German maidens	Hitler Youth	Physical education		
f) Boys	Military drill	History		
g) Education	Three 'K's'	Women		

3. Identify which of the following statements is a cause, an event or an effect. Organise them in the following table to describe their historical sequence.

a) A Nazi official in Paris was murdered by a Jew.

b) The SS organised the systematic destruction of shops and the burning of synagogues.

c) Children were indoctrinated with Nazi ideas.

d) In 1935 the Nuremberg Laws were passed.

e) The Jews were denied German citizenship.

f) Göring forced the Jews to pay a fine for the damage caused by *Kristallnacht*.

g) Hitler wanted to control the lives of young people.

h) Teachers had to be members of the Nazi Party.

i) Hitler blamed the Jews for the German defeat in the First World War and the subsequent economic crises.

Causes	Events	Effects

Checklist

How well do you know and understand the following topics?

- Nazi policies towards women.
- The successes and failures of these policies.
- Nazi policies towards the young.
- Nazi attempts to reduce unemployment.
- The Nazi economic policies.
- The standard of living under the Nazis.
- Nazi racial policies.
- Nazi policies towards minorities including the Jews.
- The Final Solution.

Student tip

You will impress examiners with precise knowledge and details of events, which could include statistics, names and dates. For example, candidates often give generalised statements about the fall in unemployment, such as 'Hitler managed to get rid of unemployment in Germany'. More precise knowledge would be 'Unemployment in Germany fell from 6 million in 1933 to about 300,000 in 1939'.

Plenary activities

Work in small groups. Imagine it is 1933 and you work at the Nazi Ministry of Education. What changes will you make to the following school timetable and extract from a history textbook?

School timetable for boys

Lessons	1	2	3	4	5
Subject	German	Science	Maths	History	Domestic Science

School timetable for girls

Lessons	1	2	3	4	5
Subject	Maths	History	Science	German	Geography

An extract from a history textbook written before the Nazis came to power.

In November 1918 the Republic had no choice but to agree to the armistice. In January 1919, Germany had its first democratic republic, which gave the German people much freedom and many rights. The Weimar Republic then had no choice but to sign the Treaty of Versailles and had to make crippling reparations payments. These payments led to the hyperinflation of 1923. In the same year an extreme party, the Nazis, led by a strange individual called Adolf Hitler, failed miserably in its attempt to seize power in Munich. Hitler actually ran away from the gun battle between his supporters and the police.

Mini exam paper

Section A

1 Study Source A

Source A: A photograph of a Hitler Youth rally at Nuremberg in 1933.

Give **TWO** things that can you learn from the photograph about the appeal of the Nazi Party in the 1930s. (4 marks)

2 The boxes below name two groups.

Choose ONE and explain the importance of that group's work for the success of the Nazi Party. (9 marks)

The SA 1923–1934 (Brownshirts)	The SS 1934–1945

Answer **EITHER** Question 3 **OR** Question 4

EITHER

3 Why was the Weimar Republic unpopular in the years 1919–1923? (12 marks)

> You may use the following in your answer and any other information of your own.
> • 1919 Treaty of Versailles
> • 1920 The Kapp Putsch
> • 1923 Hyperinflation

This is in capital letters because it is really important that you remember to give two things and not just one.

This question is only worth 4 marks. This means that you spend no more than 6 minutes on it – do not waste time that you might need later by going into too much detail! Two sentences are all you need to write.

You will always be given a choice for this question.

Note the key words in this question (**unpopular** and **why**) and the **years**. You will not get credit for any information you put which is outside of this period.

You will always be given a source in Question 1. Make sure you study it carefully as you will need to use it to answer the question. Whatever you mention must be in the source and **not** just come from your own knowledge.

It is really important that you DO NOT just write everything you know about one of these. You need to concentrate on what the question asks you – underline the key word in the question – in this case the examiner wants to know what the group contributed to Nazi success.

This information is here to help you! This means that these three points will be relevant to the question. You do not have to use any of the bullet points, and you will not lose marks for leaving any of them out, but you should mention them if you can. It does not mean that is all you need to write though – if you can think of other reasons then add those too!

These questions are worth 12 marks so it is important that you spend more time on them (about 18 minutes). You might want to jot a few ideas down before you write.

OR

4 Why was the Weimar Republic able to survive in the years 1924–1929? (12 marks)

> You may use the following in your answer and any other information of your own.
> * November 1923 Rentenmark issued
> * 1924 Dawes Plan
> * 1929 Young Plan

Section A total = 25 marks

Section B

Answer **EITHER** Question 5 **OR** Question 6

You must answer both parts of the question you choose.

EITHER

5 (a) Describe the ways in which the Nazi Party was able to win support from different groups in Germany in the years 1929–1932. (9 marks)

(b) Why was Hitler able to gain complete power in governing Germany in the years 1933–1934? Explain your answer. (16 marks)

> You may use the following in your answer and any other information of your own.
> * In January 1933, a coalition government with Hitler as Chancellor was formed.
> * In February 1933, a Dutch communist was arrested and charged with setting fire to the Reichstag.
> * In August 1934, President Hindenburg died.

OR

6 (a) Describe the role played by women in the Nazi state in the years 1933–1945. (9 marks)

(b) In what ways did the Nazi treatment of Jews change in the years 1933–1939? Explain your answer. (16 marks)

> You may use the following in your answer and any other information of your own.
> * **1933** One-day boycott of Jewish shops
> * **1935** Nuremberg Laws passed
> * **1938** *Kristallnacht*

These directions are important. Make sure that you read all four questions **and** that you can answer both parts of the question before you make your choice. Remember that question (b) carries the most marks.

Pick out the key words in the questions. In this case they are **describe the ways** and **able to win support from different groups**. Many students lose marks because they do not read the questions properly.

This question is worth a lot of marks! Make sure that you leave enough time for it – around 24 minutes.

Again, this information is here for a reason – to help you! Do not ignore it. On the other hand, if you have more information it is important that you write it in your answer as you will not be able to get excellent marks using this information **alone**.

Take note of the years in **all** questions. Any information you write that is outside the period will not gain you any marks. In this case, you might be tempted to write about the Final Solution but this would gain you no marks as it is **after** 1939.

3 Why was the Weimar Republic unpopular in the years 1919–1923? (12 marks)

Student answer	Examiner comments	Improved student answer
The Weimar Republic was unpopular in the years 1919–1923 for many reasons. The Treaty of Versailles was signed by the Weimar Government in June 1919 and this ended the First World War. The treaty meant that Germany lost land such as Alsace and Lorraine and was not allowed to build up an army. It also meant that Germany accepted the blame for starting the war. Germany was told to pay millions of marks in reparations, which it could not afford.	The candidate begins this answer well and gives some good detail on the different clauses of the Treaty of Versailles. To get to the highest marks, the answer needs to link this information to the question, which is about the Weimar Republic.	The Weimar Republic was unpopular because it had signed the Treaty of Versailles, even the most hated clause of all – the War Guilt clause. The German people bitterly resented their government's acceptance of the Treaty.
There were many groups who were opposed to the Weimar Republic. These included the Spartacists who tried to seize power in 1919 and the Nazis. In 1920 the Kapp Putsch happened where *Freikorps* tried to take over the government. This proves the unpopularity of the Weimar Republic.	The candidate shows some knowledge of the different opposition groups and, importantly, shows that this illustrates the unpopularity of Weimar. However, there is not much information on the Kapp Putsch. The candidate shows some knowledge of the different opposition groups, but more needs to be said about why these groups did not like the government. For example, the answer could add to the statement on the Kapp Putsch.	The Weimar Republic was unpopular with the army because by its acceptance of the Treaty it had agreed to weaken the army considerably, reducing its size to 100,000 and disbanding the *Freikorps*.
The biggest challenge to the Republic came in 1923. Germany had not been able to keep up the reparations payments demanded by the Versailles Treaty and this led to French troops occupying the most industrial part of Germany; the Ruhr. Inflation increased as workers went on strike and the government printed more and more bank notes. By November the German mark was worthless and many people lost their savings.	Again, the detail here is good but the candidate does not link hyperinflation with unpopularity. The detail here is good, but to get higher marks the candidate needs to link hyperinflation with the government's unpopularity. More of the effects of hyperinflation could be explained to show why this increased the unpopularity of Weimar.	By November the German mark was worthless and many people lost their life savings. The middle classes were badly hit, and they particularly resented the government – but all those who suffered felt the disaster proved that the Weimar government could not run the country well.

6 (b) In what ways did the Nazi treatment of Jews change in the years 1933–1939? Explain your answer. **(16 marks)**
You may use the following in your answer and any other information of your own:
- 1933: One-day boycott of Jewish shops
- 1935: Nuremberg Laws passed
- 1938: *Kristallnacht*.

In 1933 the Nazis organised a one-day boycott of Jewish shops. In 1934 Jews were banned from some public places such as parks and swimming pools. The Nuremberg Laws in 1935 denied Jews the right of citizenship in Germany. They also made it illegal for Jews to marry non-Jews.	The candidate shows some good knowledge here. The Nuremberg Laws have been explained and other information has been added. But the information about the boycott is simply taken from the material given in the question, so it will not be given any marks. Marks can be gained by adding detail about the boycott and linking it to change.	In 1933 the Nazis organised a one-day boycott of Jewish shops. This was one of the first examples of change – they began to discriminate against Jewish owners of businesses. In 1937 this discrimination increased and many businesses were taken away from Jews altogether.
In 1936 Jewish people lost jobs when they were banned from being vets, doctors and accountants.	A more direct comment about change is needed. This answer simply lists all the actions taken against the Jews.	In 1936 discrimination grew when Jews were excluded from professional occupations. They could not become vets, doctors or accountants.
In November 1938 *Kristallnacht* took place. Thousands of Jewish shop windows were smashed, synagogues were set on fire and some were totally destroyed. Ninety-one Jews were killed and 2,000 were arrested.	The answer gives accurate information. The best answers will go on to show that the candidate has thought about the way the treatment of Jews changed.	This was a big change – in a terror campaign against the Jews involving much more violence than ever before. Treatment of the Jews changed in 1933–1939 from increasing discrimination to outright violence against them and their property.

Don't Panic Zone

As you get close to completing your revision, the Big Day will be getting nearer and nearer. Many students find this the most stressful time and tend to go into panic mode, either working long hours without really giving their brains a chance to absorb information. or giving up and staring blankly at the wall.

Panicking simply makes your brain seize up and you find that information and thoughts simply cannot flow naturally. You become distracted and anxious, and things seem worse than they are. Many students build the exams up into more than they are. Remember: the exams are not trying to catch you out! If you have studied the course, there will be no surprises on the exam paper!

Student tip

I know how silly it is to panic, especially if you've done the work and know your stuff. I was asked by a teacher to produce a report on a project I'd done, and I panicked so much I spent the whole afternoon crying and worrying. I asked other people for help, but they were panicking too. In the end, I calmed down and looked at the task again. It turned out to be quite straightforward and, in the end, I got my report finished first and it was the best of them all!

In the exam you don't have much time, so you can't waste it by panicking. The best way to control panic is simply to do what you have to do. Think carefully for a few minutes, then start writing and as you do, the panic will drain away.

ExamZone

You will have an hour and a quarter for this exam paper and in that time you have to answer four questions. Everyone needs to answer questions 1 and 2 and then you have a choice between question 3 or 4 and then another choice between 5 or 6.

Each question is worth a different amount of marks and it is important that you use your time effectively – don't waste precious time on question 1, which is worth only 4 marks, as that might leave you with not very much time to spend on question 5b or 6b (depending on your choice), which is worth 16 marks!

Don't panic

Meet the exam paper

This diagram shows the front cover of the exam paper. These instructions, information and advice will always appear on the front of the paper. It is worth reading it carefully now. Check you understand it. Now is a good opportunity to ask your teacher about anything you are not sure of here.

Print your surname here, and your other names afterwards. This is an additional safeguard to ensure that the exam board awards the marks to the right candidate.

Here you fill in the school's exam number.

Ensure that you understand exactly how long the examination will last, and plan your time accordingly.

Note that the quality of your written communication will also be marked. Take particular care to present your thoughts and work at the highest standard you can, for maximum marks.

Here you fill in your personal exam number. Take care when writing it down because the number is important to the exam board when writing your score.

In this box, the examiner will write the total marks you have achieved in the exam paper.

Make sure that you understand exactly which questions from which sections you should attempt.

Don't feel that you have to fill the answer space provided. Everybody's handwriting varies, so a long answer from you may take up as much space a short answer from someone else.

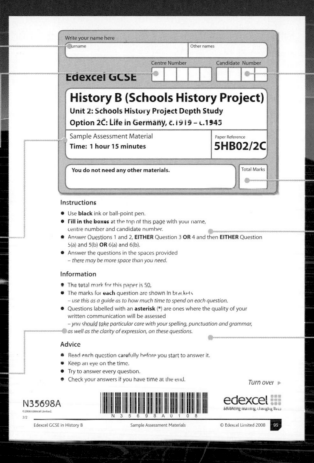

Write your name here
Surname   Other names

Centre Number   Candidate Number

Edexcel GCSE

History B (Schools History Project)
Unit 2: Schools History Project Depth Study
Option 2C: Life in Germany, c.1919 – c.1945

Sample Assessment Material   Paper Reference
Time: 1 hour 15 minutes   **5HB02/2C**

You do not need any other materials.   Total Marks

Instructions
- Use **black** ink or ball-point pen.
- **Fill in the boxes** at the top of this page with your name, centre number and candidate number.
- Answer Questions 1 and 2, **EITHER** Question 3 **OR** 4 and then **EITHER** Question 5(a) and 5(b) **OR** 6(a) and 6(b).
- Answer the questions in the spaces provided
  – there may be more space than you need.

Information
- The total mark for this paper is 50.
- The marks for **each** question are shown in brackets
  – use this as a guide as to how much time to spend on each question.
- Questions labelled with an **asterisk** (*) are ones where the quality of your written communication will be assessed
  – you should take particular care with your spelling, punctuation and grammar, as well as the clarity of expression, on these questions.

Advice
- Read each question carefully before you start to answer it.
- Keep an eye on the time.
- Try to answer every question.
- Check your answers if you have time at the end.

Turn over ▶

N35698A

2/2
Edexcel GCSE in History B   Sample Assessment Materials   © Edexcel Limited 2008   95

edexcel
advancing learning, changing lives

Understanding the language of the exam paper

Outline	Provide more than one point or reason. At least two or more reasons are necessary to reach Level 3
Describe	The examiner is looking for a concise and organised account. Jot down three or four points in the margin that you want to include in your answer. Arrange them in the most logical order
Explain how	The examiner is trying to discover whether you understand the key events in Germany's history c1919–c1945, and why they happened. The more detail you can give, the more marks you will receive
Give reasons for your answer	You need to provide an explanation
Do you agree?	You are free to agree or disagree. What makes a difference is how well you back up your case

Zone Out

This section provides answers to the most common questions students have about what happens after they complete their exams. For more information, visit www.heinemann.co.uk/hotlinks (express code 4448P) and click on examzone.

About your grades

Whether you've done better than, worse than, or just as you expected, your grades are the final measure of your performance on your course and in the exams. On this page we explain some of the information that appears on your results slip and tell you what to do if you think something is wrong. We answer the most popular questions about grades and look at some of the options facing you.

When will my results be published?

Results for summer examinations are issued on the **middle** two Thursdays in August, with GCE first and GCSE second. January exam results are issued in March.

Can I get my results online?

Visit www.heinemann.co.uk/hotlinks (express code 4448P) and click on Results Plus, where you will find detailed student results information including the 'Edexcel Gradeometer', which demonstrates how close you were to the nearest grade boundary.

I haven't done as well as I expected. What can I do now?

First of all, talk to your subject teacher. After all the teaching that you have had, tests and internal examinations, he/she is the person who best knows what grade you are capable of achieving. Take your results slip to your subject teacher, and go through the information on it in detail. If you both think there is something wrong with the result, the school or college can apply to see your completed examination paper and then, if necessary, ask for a re-mark immediately. The original mark can be confirmed or lowered, as well as raised, as a result of a re-mark.

How do my grades compare with those of everybody else who sat this exam?

You can compare your results with those of others in the UK who have completed the same examination using the information on the Edexcel website accessed at www.heinemann.co.uk/hotlinks (express code 4448P) by clicking on Edexcel.

I achieved a higher mark for the same unit last time. Can I use that result?

Yes. The higher score is the one that goes towards your overall grade. Even if you sat a unit more than twice, the best result will be used automatically when the overall grade is calculated. You do not need to ask the exam board to take into account a previous result. This will be done automatically so you can be assured that all your best unit results have gone into calculating your overall grade.

What happens if I was ill over the period of my examinations?

If you become ill before or during the examination period you are eligible for special consideration. This also applies if you have been affected by an accident, bereavement or serious disturbance during an examination.

If my school has requested special consideration for me, is this shown on my Statement of Results?

If your school has requested special consideration for you, it is not shown on your results slip, but it will be shown on a subject mark report that is sent to your school or college. If you want to know whether special consideration was requested for you, you should ask your Examinations Officer.

Can I have a re-mark of my examination paper?

Yes, this is possible, but remember that only your school or college can apply for a re-mark, not you or your parents/carers. First of all, you should consider carefully whether or not to ask your school or college to make a request for a re-mark. It is worth knowing that very few re-marks result in a change to a grade – not because Edexcel is embarrassed that a change of marks has been made, but simply because a re-mark request has shown that the original marking was accurate. Check the closing date for re-marking requests with your Examinations Officer.

When I asked for a re-mark of my paper, my subject grade went down. What can I do?

There is no guarantee that your grades will go up if your papers are re-marked. They can also go down or stay the same. After a re-mark, the only way to improve your grade is to take the examination again. Your school or college Examinations Officer can tell you when you can do that.

How many times can I re-sit a unit?

You may re-sit a modular GCSE Science or Mathematics module test once, prior to taking your terminal examination and before obtaining your final overall grade. The highest score obtained on either the first attempt or the re-sit counts towards your final grade. If you enter a module in GCSE Mathematics at a different tier, this does not count as a re-sit. If you are on the full modular History GCSE course, and sat the first unit last year, you may re-sit module 1 when you sit module 2 to maximise your full course grade.

For much more information, go to www.heinemann.co.uk/hotlinks (express code 4448P) and click on examzone.

Glossary

This Glossary contains all the key words used in the book. When appropriate the definitions are particularly directed to the period being studied.

Anti-Semitism – Opposition to and attacks on Jews.
Armistice – Ceasefire.
Aryan – Nazi term for someone of supposedly Germanic stock.
Autarky – Self-sufficiency.
Autobahns – German motorways.

Censorship – When unacceptable parts, or whole books, films, etc, are officially suppressed.
Coalition – A government by two or more political parties.
Concentration camps – Prisons where inmates were treated with great brutality.
Concordat – Agreement.
Conscription – Compulsory military service.
Constitution – System of rules by which a country is governed.

Democracy – Where people choose the government from two or more parties.
Dictatorship – One-party state governed by one person who has total control.

Edelweiss – This flower was the symbol on the badges worn by members of the Edelweiss Pirates. It also means noble or white.
Eugenics – Study of improving the quality of the human race.

Final Solution – The Nazi policy to exterminate all Jews in Europe.
Fuhrer – German for leader.

Gestapo – Nazi secret police.
Ghetto – An area of a city or town used for one racial group.

Hyperinflation – When prices go up very quickly.

Indoctrination – Brainwashing people into accepting ideas.
Invisible unemployed – Unemployed not counted in official figures.

Judiciary – Judges.

Kaiser – Emperor.

Labour exchanges – Job centres.
Lebensraum – Living space.

Orator – A fluent and effective public speaker.

Passive resistance – To resist authority in a peaceful, non-violent way.
Police state – A totalitarian state controlled by a political police force.
Propaganda – False or misleading information given out to spread certain points of view.
Purge – To remove enemies by terror.
Putsch – An uprising, an attempt to overthrow the government.

Real wages – Wages adjusted to allow for inflation.
Rearmament – Building up armed forces and weapons.
Reichstag – Parliament.
Reparations – Compensation for war damages paid by a defeated state.
The Ruhr – The industrial part of Germany producing coal, iron and steel.

Spartacists – The name of the German Communist Party.
The SS – Originally the private bodyguard for Hitler, but later the organisation that removed opposition to the Nazi government.
State parliament – Each German state, such as Bavaria and Saxony, elected its own parliament.

Third Reich – Third empire.

Untermenschen – German word for sub-humans, including Jews and Slavs.

Wall Street Crash – Wall Street is the name of the New York Stock Exchange. Share prices fell disastrously on Wall Street in October 1929.

Index

In the following index, main entries of key words are given in bold type and the first page number that is also in bold will lead you to a definition of the word. For further definitions of unfamiliar words, see the Glossary on page 110.